Modern Communication with Social Media

A Simplified Primer to Communication and Social Media

by

Mamta Dalal

FIRST EDITION 2019
Copyright © BPB Publications, India
ISBN: 978-93-88511-841

Distributors:

BPB PUBLICATIONS
20, Ansari Road, Darya Ganj
New Delhi-110002
Ph: 23254990/23254991

DECCAN AGENCIES
4-3-329, Bank Street,
Hyderabad-500195
Ph: 24756967/24756400

MICRO MEDIA
Shop No. 5, Mahendra Chambers,
150 DN Rd. Next to Capital Cinema,
V.T. (C.S.T.) Station, MUMBAI-400 001
Ph: 22078296/22078297

BPB BOOK CENTRE
376 Old Lajpat Rai Market,
Delhi-110006
Ph: 23861747

Published by Manish Jain for BPB Publications, 20 Ansari Road, Darya Ganj, New Delhi-110002 and Printed at Repro India Ltd, Mumbai

About the Author

Mamta Dalal works in the technology industry and is proficient in various technologies and products. She is based in Mumbai, India. When not busy at work, she can be found engrossed in books, movies, and shows.

Acknowledgement

I would like to thank my family, especially my mother, my husband, and in-laws for their utmost support and encouragement always. I would also like to thank the team at BPB Publications for their kind guidance and support.

Preface

This book, **Modern Communication with Social Media**, explores the evolution of communication, and communication media, and covers social media in detail. It examines some of the most popular social media platforms available today. The book concludes with an analysis of various social media management tools.

Disclaimer: The landscape of software platforms, especially social media platforms is constantly changing with new tools arriving every other day, and new updates are being made to existing social media platforms with lightning speed. In such a scenario, it is not possible to cover every feature of such platforms, for they may not exist in the near future. This book is a primer and only aims to introduce the major features of each platform/tool. By the time you read this book, it is possible that there may be several new updates to the tool/platform.

Errata

We take immense pride in our work at BPB Publications and follow best practices to ensure the accuracy of our content to provide with an indulging reading experience to our subscribers. Our readers are our mirrors, and we use their inputs to reflect and improve upon human errors if any, occurred during the publishing processes involved. To let us maintain the quality and help us reach out to any readers who might be having difficulties due to any unforeseen errors, please write to us at:

errata@bpbonline.com

Your support, suggestions and feedbacks are highly appreciated by the BPB Publications' Family.

Table of Contents

CHAPTER 1
Communication

In this chapter, we shall learn about communication.

Objectives

By the end of this chapter, you will be able to:

- Identify the need for communication
- Trace the history and growth of communication
- Understand the basics of communication
- Identify the various forms of communication
- Understand different types of communication

Communication -Definition

Communication is defined as the exchange of information from one entity/person to another (one or many). Communication can be one-way, two- way, or a broadcast (in which the same message is transmitted to many people). The process of communication may involve words, signs, symbols, behavioral signs, and more.

Need for communication

Communication is essential to most, if not all, forms of living organisms. Different creatures communicate in different ways.

Figure 1.1: Communication in the Animal Kingdom

The howling of wolves, barking of dogs, and croaking of frogs are all varied forms of communication. This is their way of communicating with each other and the world.

Yet other forms of communication may not be as obvious. Take for example, bird formations such as a flock of starlings gathering in unison at dusk.

All the birds in the flock move in synchronicity. The exact direction in which to turn is communicated from one bird to several of its nearest neighbors.

Figure 1.2: Communication Among Birds

Birds may communicate through sound or even through non-vocal signals such as by beating the air with their wings.

Why is communication necessary?

Communication in the animal (and bird) kingdom is needed for various reasons - to warn one another of approaching danger, to find food, to seek a mate, to fend off a rival or nemesis, and so on. For example, bees dance when they find nectar. The scout bee will dance in the hive, thus drawing other bees to the location of the nectar. Communication among animals can happen through a variety of signals.

Figure 1.3: Communication Conveying Danger/Fear

Just as the animal kingdom needs communication, so does mankind.

Tracing the evolution of communication

As humans gradually evolved from the stone age to the present age, so did the way they communicated with one another.

The early years

Early man communicated via drawings and paintings on stone. Cave paintings created during this period of human evolution, classified as Paleolithic Period, were the first kind of recorded communication that could be seen in history. Stone tools were being used not just for hunting prey or butchering animals for food, but also for communicating with one another.

Later, during the Bronze Age, the period of time between the Stone Age and the Iron Age, when bronze was used widely to make tools and weapons, was also the period when the Sumerians developed the *first known forms of written communication.*

The Bronze Age in Sumer is estimated to be approximately 3700 BC. Around the same time, approximately 3100 BC, independent writing systems also arose in Egypt, but it is not clear if they were inspired by Sumer or were formed on their own.

The ancient Sumerians are also said to be the first known accountants, since they invented scripts for rudimentary accounting. They developed a form of writing called cuneiform, which went on to be used until the first century AD. The writing was made on clay tablets using blunt tools such as reeds, which were then baked in the sun. Refer *Figure 1.4* which shows an ancient clay tablet.

Figure 1.4: Ancient Clay Tablet

The cuneiform script underwent extensive changes over a period of more than two millennia.

From tablets to early paper

Ancient Egyptians used paper made from the Papyrus plant to create writing for business and trade. They made use of a reed pen to write on paper, so their writing was more fluid. Gradually ancient scripts evolved from pictographic styles toward Phoenician or alphabetic styles. Different forms of alphabet systems began to be discovered across the world by different civilizations. For example, the Greek alphabet was invented around late 9th or early 8th century BC. Communication became more improved with the invention of the alphabet system.

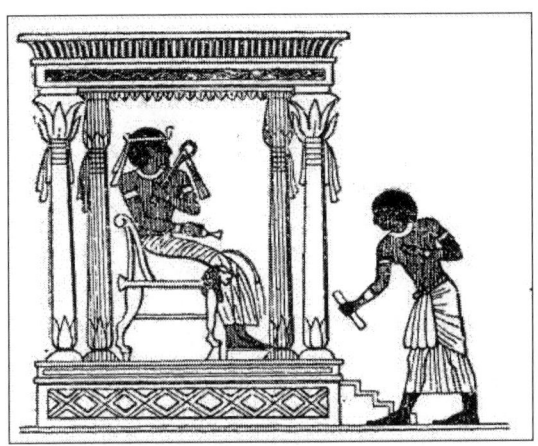

Figure 1.5: Ancient Message Carrier

The word courier (a message carrier) means runner, and comes from the Latin word *currere*, which means to *run*. In the year 490 BC, a Greek named Pheidippides is said to have run all the way from Marathon to Athens, to announce the victory of Greek over Persia. Back in that era, it was common for dedicated, highly trained runners to cover long distances by foot to convey royal commands, military orders, legal summons, and other kind of messages.

Persian messengers of the Turkish sultan ran regularly from Constantinople to Adrianople, covering 200 miles, in two days and nights. In the early 13th century, couriers of the Inca civilization in ancient Peru used a relay system to deliver not just messages, but also fruit, fish, and meat from the coast to the mountain villages. The relay messengers traveled by foot, often across the Inca rope bridges.

Ancient Greeks also used carrier pigeons to transmit messages. Over the centuries, Romans, Greeks, Persians, French, Mughal, and other empires have regularly employed pigeons for communication. Even until recently, many regions still used pigeons to transmit materials across difficult terrain.

Other different channels of communication also began to evolve. Horses, mules, and donkeys were often used to transport messengers from one place to another. Makeshift boats and rafts began to be developed to transport messages across water.

Advent of paper and paper-based communication

Papermaking was first documented in China during 25–220 AD and thereafter spread across Asia. Later, around the 8th century, the technique of Chinese papermaking was adopted by the Middle East after they mined it from their Chinese prisoners of war. The Middle Easterners developed pulp mills and paper mills to manufacture paper. Paper also reached India by around the 7th century and then Europe by the 11th century.

The concept of bulletins and announcements existed from the time of the ancient Greeks and Romans. However, the first true newspapers made a mark only after Johannes Gutenberg presented his movable type printing press in Europe around 1440. The first weekly newspaper, called Relation aller Fürnemmen und gedenckwürdigen Historien, was published in Germany by Johann Carolus in 1604. In 1650, the first daily newspaper, the Einkommende Zeitung, was published.

Growth of electromechanical communication

The telegraph era was ushered in the 1840s in the United States when Samuel Morse and his associates launched the electrical telegraph system. However, a long-distance communication system connecting various states of America was still a work in progress. During that time, from April 3, 1860 to October 1861, a mail service system of dedicated horse riders called the Pony Express became the American West's primary means of communication. This mail service used a relay system, allowing riders to rest or switch mounts at established stations.

Figure 1.6: *Horse Riders Carrying Mail*

Around 1861, the first transcontinental telegraph was completed, enabling greater communication. Then came the telephone. Though several people during that era were working on devices like the telephone, it is Alexander Graham Bell, who in 1876, received the first US patent for his electric telephone. Later by around 1915, transcontinental telephone service was established, enabling people to communicate across the continents. The invention and spread of the telephone went on to change the lives of people all over the world. Today, we can't imagine a life without a telephone, be it a landline or a smartphone.

In 1927, television was launched, ushering a new revolution in mass media and communication.

The information and digital age

The era of 1940s onwards witnessed rapid growth in communication technology. It was around 1940 that the first large-scale automatic digital computer in the United States called the Mark 1 was created by Harvard University. Later, in 1963, the first ever geosynchronous communications satellite was launched. Electronic mail or Email, a novel approach to send text messages electronically, was first used in 1965 at MIT. 1969 witnessed the launch of the **Advanced Research Projects Agency Network (ARPANET)** which in turn eventually led to the birth of the Internet.

By late 1970, personal computers were launched. In 1981, the world´s first automatic mobile phone, the *Nordic Mobile Telephone*, was created.

Around 1994, came the emergence of the World Wide Web; followed soon after by real time messaging or Internet chat. IRC, ICQ, and AOL were the most popular Internet chat platforms in the nineties. A couple of years later, blogging was invented and then came social networking. As of today, our world is a highly connected one.

Figure 1.7: Social Networking

Modern communication is the communication in the digital age where the communication takes place through electronic and digital channels.

Forms of communication

There are various forms of communication today, such as:

Mass Communication	Interpersonal Communication	Organizational Communication
• Involves transfer of a message or information to a large audience. • Television and radio channels are traditional means of broadcast for mass communication.	• Involves transfer or message from one person to another.	• Involves communication within an organization, typically from managers to the employees.

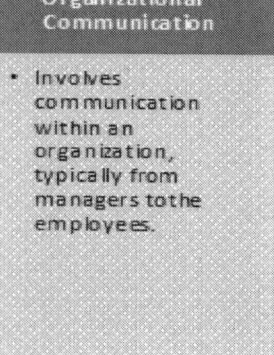

Interpersonal communication can be categorized as synchronous and asynchronous.

Examples of synchronous communication (where the parties are present) can include in-person or face-to-face chats and telephone conversations.

Figure 1.8: Face-to-face Chats

Examples of asynchronous communication are text messages and emails that can be sent and received at different points in time.

Figure 1.9: Texting and Emailing

Types of Communication

Primarily, three types of communication exist. These are as follows:

Verbal/oral communication	• involving listening to a person to understand the meaning of a message
Non-verbal communication	• involving observing a person and inferring meaning.
Written communication	• in which a message is read.

Verbal Communication

In verbal communication, the medium is oral. This type of communication may take place over the phone or in person. A conversation with a friend, an enquiry put to the teller at the bank counter, an office meeting to brainstorm ideas, an announcement over the loudspeaker at the local train station - all these are examples of verbal communication.

Figure 1.10: Brainstorming

Nonverbal Communication

Nonverbal communication can take place through a variety of cues that can support or detract from a sender's message. Some of these include body language, eye contact, touch gestures, facial expressions, and posture. Defiance or non-cooperation can for example be shown without any verbal communication just through eye contact and body language. Likewise, appreciation or approval can be shown through a nod, a thumbs up sign, or through applause.

Effective communication requires body language, appearance, and tone to be in sync with the words one is trying to convey.

Written Communication

Written communications are handwritten, printed, or typed messages. Examples of written communications include emails, letters, notes, and so on.

With the digital age, traditional forms of verbal, nonverbal and written communication have been changed. Earlier, verbal communication used to be synchronous and written communication usually asynchronous. That is, the sender would write a message that the receiver could read at any time, even days later. Now, in modern communication, even a verbal message such as a voice note sent through a smartphone can be heard days later, not necessarily in real time. Similarly, a written message such as a chat message can be instant, with the recipient reading within seconds after the sender has transmitted it. Thus, the written communication becomes synchronous whereas the verbal can become asynchronous.

Summary

- Communication is essential to living beings for a variety of reasons.
- Communication is defined as the exchange of information from one entity/person to another (one or many).
- Communication can be one-way, two-way, or a broadcast (in which the same message is transmitted to many persons).

- Three major forms of communication are: mass communication, interpersonal communication, and organizational communication.
- Communication can be classified as verbal, non-verbal, and written.

Chapter 1 Quiz

1. Pony Express was the name of a mail service commonly used in ancient Peru. [True/False]

2. ARPANET stands for _____.

3. Telephone conversations are an example of [synchronous/asynchronous] communication.

4. Eye contact is an example of _____ [verbal/non-verbal communication].

CHAPTER 2
Communication Channels

In this chapter, we shall learn about communication channels, their purpose and types.

Objectives

By the end of this chapter, you will be able to:

- Define a communication channel
- Identify various communication channels

Communication Channels - Definition

A communication channel is a medium used to communicate a message. For example, television is a popular mass communication channel that can broadcast a message to masses of people simultaneously.

The choice of communication channel can determine the effectiveness of the message. Different communication channels are more or less effective at transmitting different kinds of information. The key to effective communication is to match the communication channel with the goal of the message. Choosing the right or appropriate communication channel can also depend on the audience.

Figure 2.1: *Communication Channels*

Types of Communication Channels

Various types of communication channels exist today. Some of these include the following:

- Face-to-face conversation
- Telephonic conversations
- Text messages (SMS)
- Emails
- Video calls
- Voice notes
- Letters, memos, or notes
- Video conference calls
- Blogs
- Official printed documents
- Mobile app notifications
- Mass media channels such as television, radio, Websites, social media networks, and so on

Not all channels are meant for every kind of communication. They vary from need to need, and audience to audience.

Let's look at a few examples of different communication channels and the kind of messages they communicate.

For example, a voice note to your friend informing him of a newly released movie is different from a crisis alert from a mobile weather app notifying you of a looming cyclone that could hit your town. The former is just information and not necessarily urgent. The latter is an urgent and probably lifesaving message.

Knowing that your town could be the first to be hit drastically by a cyclone can help you plan for immediate evacuation and safety measures.

Likewise, a text message informing a friend who is waiting for you to join her that you will be late in arriving, is different from a manager sending an appreciation -mail to his team. In the former scenario, an email could be too formal, a phone call or a text would be more suitable.

It is important to understand the channels and knowing how to use them is critical for effective communication.

Face to face communication and telephonic conversations are crucial in scenarios like when a sender is conveying a sense or emotional message needs feedback immediately. Also, in such types of communication, there is no record of the conversation, unless one uses an answering machine for the calls.

Text messages are often used for short, quick communication. Text messages could again be formal or informal. Formal text messages could be a bank alert message, an advertiser sending promotional messages, and so on. Examples of informal messages could be exchange of messages between family and friends.

Written communication is often preferred when the sender wants a record of the communication, does not require an urgent response, and/or, is physically separated from the receiver. Written communication too can be formal or informal. For example, a letter from a principal of a school to parents of a student, an announcement from a manager to his employees can be classified as formal written communication. In businesses, letters are important documents.

A letter from a husband to his wife or vice versa or a letter from one sibling to another are examples of informal written communication.

These days, however, people prefer email over written communication, for both formal and informal communication.

Figure 2.2: *Email*

Official documents can be sent within minutes through emails, establishing an effective business to business relationship. Emails can also be preserved as an evidence of communication. Applying for jobs has become easier because of emails. Email is also a key tool for online marketing these days.

According to the study conducted by the research group Radicati **(https://www.radicati.com/wp/wp-content/uploads/2015/02/Email-Statistics-Report-2015-2019-Executive-Summary.pdf),** email will be used by 3 billion people by 2020. 1.6 billion people still don't have electricity. So, with time if more people receive electricity, the number of email users is expected to grow higher. As per the study report, the number of emails sent and received per day is expected to reach 246 billion by the end of 2019. This shows how pervasive the use of email has become.

Video conference calls are used when two or more participants in a communication who are situated far apart, want to have face time while they communicate.

Figure 2.3: Video Conference Call

Image Courtesy:
https://www.flickr.com/photos/wolfvision_vsolution/14472241106

For example, a manager sitting in Tokyo wants to discuss an important matter with two of his colleagues who are in Delhi. They can all join a video conference call through which they can see each other in real time and communicate.

Unlike telephonic calls where the sender and receiver cannot see each other and therefore may miss nonverbal cues such as body language, in a video call, they can see each other, therefore, they have the opportunity to grasp the nonverbal signs.

Mass media channels such as television, radio, blogs, websites, and social media are used to communicate information to a wider audience. A radio message can be heard by millions of people across the world.

Likewise, a television broadcast may be watched by large numbers of people across the globe.

Figure 2.4: Television Broadcast

A blog or site can be simultaneously read by many people across the globe. For instance, a travel blog can convey travel related information to interested person who may be located anywhere, and in any time zone. Also, a blog does not have to be read in real time but can be read months or even years later.

In the current digital age, social media networks are proving even popular for news consumption than traditional media such as TV or radio.

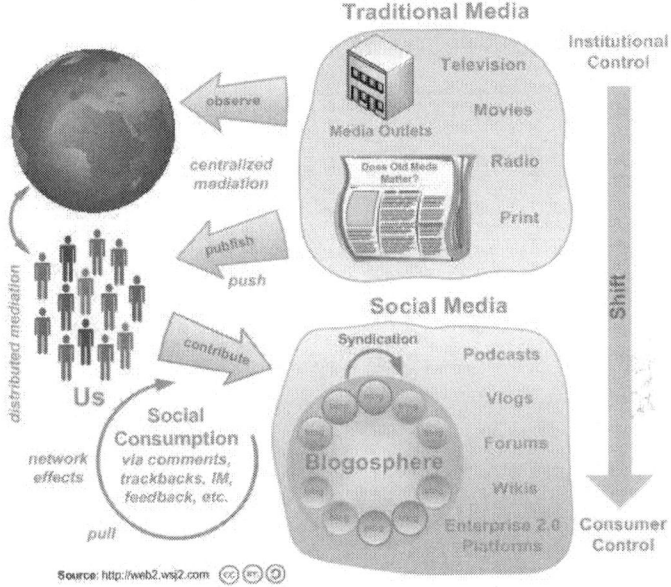

Figure 2.5: Infographic depicting rise of Social Media

Image Courtesy: **https://www.flickr.com/photos/dionh/373848076**

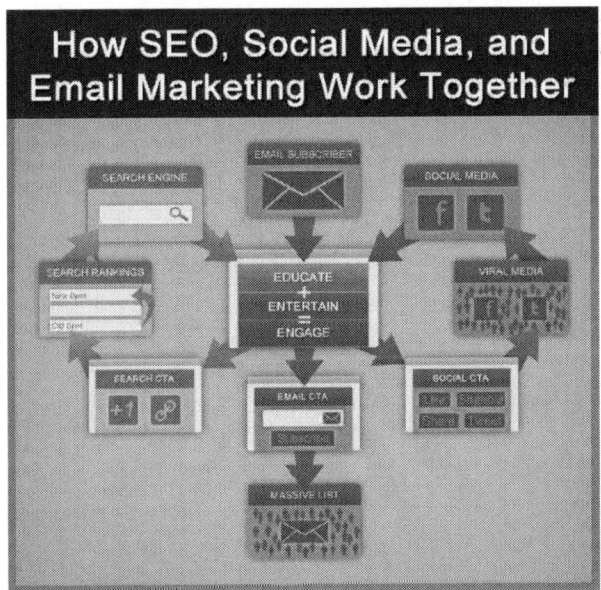

Figure 2.6: Infographic depicting SEO, social media and email marketing

The greatest benefit that social media can offer over traditional media is that people can read instant breaking news alerts on Facebook or Twitter on the go. You cannot lug your TV everywhere you go however, your phone is always with you and it's easier and faster to check the news on the phone.

Figure 2.7: Checking News on Phones

Additional Information

You can refer to the following links for additional information: **https://www.examples.com/business/formal-email.html**

http://open.lib.umn.edu/organizationalbehavior/chapter/8-4-different-types-of-communication-and-channels/

https://smallbusiness.chron.com/communication-channels-within-organization-61447.html

Summary

- A communication channel is a medium used to communicate a message.
- The choice of communication channel can determine the effectiveness of the message.
- Different communication channels are more or less effective at transmitting different kinds of information.

- The key to effective communication is to match the communication channel with the goal of the message.
- Various types of communication channels exist today, such as face-to-face conversations, telephonic conversations, text messages, emails, and more.

Chapter 2 Quiz

1. Face to face communication and telephonic conversations are crucial in scenarios like when a sender is conveying a sense or emotional message needs feedback immediately. [True/False]

2. Video conference calls are used when two or more participants in a communication, who are situated far apart, want to have face time while they communicate. [True/False]

3. A blog is used for real-time instant communication, and must be read immediately. [True/False]

CHAPTER 3
Social Media

Today, many of us have become accustomed to various kinds of apps such as Facebook, WhatsApp, and Instagram on our smartphones. While we do know that some of them are classified as social media, we may not be aware of the formal definition of social media, its evolution, and which kind of apps and sites can be classified as social media. In this chapter, we shall explore these topics.

Objectives

By the end of this chapter, you will be able to:
- Define social media
- Trace the history of social media
- Identify the features of social media
- List the benefits of social media

What is Social Media?

Social media refers to a set of Websites and applications that enable people to share various kinds of content in a quick and efficient manner, often in real-time. The content may be shared one to one, to a group, or to the online world at large.

Figure 3.1: Sharing Content with One Another

There are several other formal definitions of social media. Consider, for example, the definition from Merriam Webster:

> *"forms of electronic communication (such as websites for social networking and microblogging) through which users create online communities to share information, ideas, personal messages, and other content (such as videos)".*

At its most basic level, the main role of social media in communication is to enable people to connect with one another regardless of distance, time, and other factors.

Figure 3.2: Social Media

Top most social networks are usually available in multiple languages, not just English. They facilitate users to connect with friends or people across geographical, political or economic borders. Approximately 2 billion Internet users are using social networks today and these statistics are still expected to grow as smartphone usage gain traction, particularly in developing countries.

A brief history of social media

The first known use of this term was around 2004, although as a concept, it can be traced as far back as 1970s and 80s.

In the late 1970s, Bulletin board systems were created to allow users to log in to computer servers and upload and download software and information. Some of them also enabled users to read news and message each other.

Commonly called BBS, they became hugely popular over time and continued to be used until the late 1990s.

BBSes can be thought of as the precursors to today's social networks and social media (though the term itself had not been invented yet) since they enabled users to communicate with each other through messages, chats, and even share media.

Then, the emergence of dial-up Internet and Web browsers providing global access phased out the BBS services. Today, only a handful of BBS are active worldwide. In Taiwan, for example, a Chinese language BBS named PTT had 1.5 million registered users in 2014.

The success of BBSes further led to the emergence of instant messaging clients and relay chat software such as IRC and ICQ.

IRC

Internet Relay Chat, or IRC as it is called in short, was created in 1988 and continues to be in use even today, though its popularity has declined. As of 2003, there were 1 million users, but the numbers dropped off drastically in the subsequent years.

It was primarily created to facilitate group communication, but users can also have one-on-one messaging, called as private messaging. Additionally, users can perform data transfer and share files and media.

ICQ

ICQ (based on the phrase I Seek You), developed in 1996, was the first messaging client to offer a dedicated service with individual user accounts, focusing on one-to-one conversations.

Thus, it can be thought of as standalone instant messaging client. It was also a pioneering online instant messenger service.

ICQ was created by an Israeli company named Mirabilis. It's currently owned by a Russian Internet company called Mail.Ru.

When you signed up, you received a number called as User Identification Number, rather than a username.

In the early years, the user interface and functionality of the application were concerned, they were just basic. The application had few security or privacy settings. Unlike in today's apps, there was no setting to turn this off. Later, advanced features were added to the app such as authorization to enable or disable random users to message you, multi-user chat, SMS support, and file transfer.

In 1998, AOL acquired Mirabilis. In the immediate years following that, ICQ flourished well. However, as AOL had several other products to take care of, ICQ began to be sidelined. Soon, its popularity declined in America on account of several other instant messengers entering the market and providing stiff competition.

In April 2010, AOL sold Mirabilis to Digital Sky Technologies of Russia, which later (in September 2010) changed its name to the Mail. ru group.

After the acquisition, Mail.ru converted the app for mobile messaging and ensured its successful adoption in Russia. In 2014, the messenger reported a growth in users for the first time since several years.

SixDegrees.com

In the 90s, social networking websites were just beginning to spring up. A Website could be called as a Social Networking Site only if it satisfied these below-mentioned conditions:

- It enables you to register as a user, create a profile, and add information about yourself
- It enables you to add friends to a master list

- It allows your friends to be viewed by other users who viewed your profile

Sixdegrees.com was the first Website to fully meet all these requirements. It is often called as the first ever social media Website.

It was created by Andrew Weinreich in May 1996 and publicly launched in 1997.

The Website included several features such as personal profiles, friends lists, instant messaging, and school affiliations as one combined service.

In later years, sites like *Myspace* and *Friendster* would build upon these to offer even more features.

The Sixdegrees.com Website recorded over one million registered users. However, networks were limited because the Internet was still not widely prevalent across the globe.

In 2000, the Website was sold to YouthStream Media Networks and eventually closed in 2001.

Blogs, Instant Messengers, and the Rise of Social Media

Then, the concept of blogging emerged. This too was a form of social media. Blog hosting platforms enabled people to write long or short posts, with text and visual media.

In the subsequent years, other social networking sites such as Reddit, Tumblr, and MySpace began to emerge. Reddit was (and still is) popular for social news, discussions, and entertainment. Tumblr provides a microblogging platform.

MySpace fulfills its role in the social networking space by providing an interactive, user-submitted set-up of friends, blogs, groups, photos, music, and videos.

Influenced by the widespread popularity of IRC and ICQ, instant messaging software such as Yahoo! Messenger, AOL Messenger, Google Talk, and MSN Messenger were released and became hits worldwide.

Many Websites providing blogging capabilities came up, such as MySpace, Blogger, and GeoCities. A professional social networking platform, LinkedIn, was launched in 2003.

People then wanted to share much more than just content with others. To meet this need, photo sharing sites came into being. Flickr, Picassa Web, and PhotoBucket were among the leading photo sharing sites.

YouTube was launched in 2005 as a video sharing platform. Anyone could create and upload videos that would then be consumed by anyone across the globe. You could create videos with limited or restricted access and share a link to your video with your chosen circle of friends and family.

In mid 2000s, Facebook and Twitter were launched. They have met with unprecedented success worldwide. These sites continue to be the most popular social networks on the Internet.

At the same time, several other social networking sites such as *Tumblr, Foursquare, LinkedIn,* and Pinterest began emerging, that were designed to meet specific social networking needs. For example, the goal was, LinkedIn was unique in that it was designed for business-oriented or professional social networking.

Several hundreds of social networking sites and applications were launched but could not last for long. Lack of revenue led to shutting down of many a social networking service.

For example, *Orkut*, a social networking site, by Google was hugely popular and lasted for a good 10 years before finally closing in 2014. Another popular social networking service, Vine, that allowed people to host and share short videos lasted from 2013 to 2016. It had over 200 million users before it shut down.

As of today, people associate the term with social media apps on their smartphones or tablets, though it's not restricted to these devices alone.

The Evolution of Social Media

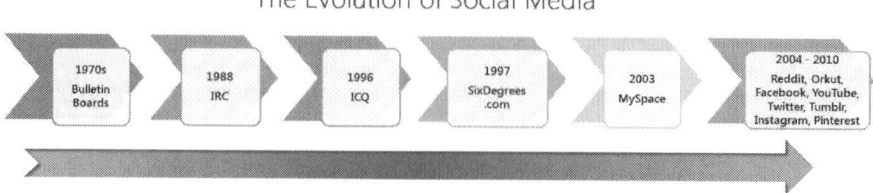

Figure 3.3: Evolution of Social Media

Features of Social Media

Figure 3.4: Features of Social Media

Most of the social media platforms exhibit certain features that are common among them:

Participatory

A good social media service or site should encourage user participation.

Community

A social media platform should facilitate creation of communities or groups. Using this feature, users can form communities or groups based on common interests, such as books, film, art, and so on. Some users who are familiar with each other in real life as friends or family can also extend it to social media to form their own community online.

Connectedness

One of the biggest USPs of a social media platform is its connectedness. Users can feel connected to one another irrespective of age, language, geography, or gender.

Building of Profiles

Social media platforms should encourage users to create their social media profile upon registration. A profile can include generic information or may even include personal information.

Sharing of Content

A social media platform should enable users to share different types of content easily and efficiently.

Conversations

A social media platform should also provide for conversations between users, as opposed to just broadcast wherein content is shared with a large audience.

Benefits of Social Media

- **Instant communication**

  Consider an example. Your friend is in Tokyo and shares a picture of the Tokyo subway on social media. You, though being miles away and in a different time zone, can see it instantly, thanks to the power of social media.

  What's more, through the new features available on social media platforms, you can indicate to him/her that you viewed the photo and liked it too! You can ask your friend for more information about the subway and receive replies instantly. Thus, regardless of time and distance, you and your friend can communicate and share in real time.

- **Real-time news**

  As and when important newsworthy events happen across the world, social media updates in real time can convey information regarding them. For example, consider Elon Musk of Tesla launching SpaceX in the US. A person sitting in a remote corner of India can learn about this event, simply by viewing the social media event.

- **Life-saving information during natural disasters**

  In recent times, social media platforms such as Facebook, Twitter, and Snapchat have become life-saving tools in the wake of natural disasters. First responders (people with specialized training who are the first to arrive and provide assistance at the scene of an emergency, such as an accident, natural disaster, or terrorist attack. They typically include paramedics, emergency medical technicians, police officers, firefighters, and so on) have been able to use information from social media to help distribute relief to areas in need of emergency assistance.

After a 7.8 magnitude earthquake hit Nepal in 2015, Facebook launched a *Safety Check* feature, allowing users to mark themselves safe in regions affected by natural disasters and emergencies and letting their near and dear ones to know that they were safe.

Google too implemented a PersonFinder feature that enables users to text the name of a loved one to a number, depending on their location, and only requires SMS, not an internet connection.

Another example: Immediately after Hurricane Harvey struck in USA, the social media platform Snapchat created a custom filter using which, the users in affected areas could use the filter and contribute to the story to help others know what was happening. Over 300,000 users contributed to the SnapStory. Snapchat's map feature also allowed people to see where the users were posting from, at any given time. This not only helped the first responders to reach there with help but also notified others, who were traveling there to stay away from affected areas.

- **Fun and entertaining**

  Social media can be fun and entertaining too! Cat pictures and videos, cute fluffy dogs, cosplay photos, funny memes, and so much more are being shared through the years, providing easy armchair entertainment. Twitter has a feature called threaded tweets that one can use to tell long stories with each tweet containing no more than 280 characters.

- **Educational**

  Social media can be a powerful tool for education. Knowledge curation becomes better through social media. Useful study tips, live science chats and stories for schools, recommendations for good books for school children - there's so much one can leverage from social media. By following and reading up dedicated educational social media accounts, school staff and parents can benefit greatly.

One of the key purposes of social media is to facilitate modern communication.

Summary

- Social media refers to a set of Websites and applications that enable people to share various kinds of content in a quick and efficient manner, often in real-time.

- The main role of social media in communication is to enable people to connect with one another regardless of distance, time, and other factors.

- Social media has a rich history. Though the first known use of the term social media was around 2004, its origins can be traced as far back as 1970s and 80s.

- Most of the social media platforms exhibit certain features that are common among them, such as enabling user participation, facilitating creation of communities or groups, connectedness, and soon.

- There are various benefits of social media, such as offering instant communication, providing real-time news, producing life-saving information during natural disasters, being a source of fun and finally, being educational.

Chapter 3 Quiz

1. A social media profile must never include personal information. [True/False]

2. Topmost social networks are usually available in multiple languages, not just English. [True/False]

3. _____ was an early messaging application in which when you signed up, you received a number called as User Identification Number, rather than a user name.

4. _____ is often called as the first ever social media Website.

5. Social media can often help to provide life-saving information during natural disasters. [True/False]

CHAPTER 4
Twitter

In this chapter, we shall explore the social media platform, Twitter.

Objectives

By the end of this chapter, you will be able to:
- Understand the basics of Twitter platform
- Identify key features of Twitter
- Create a Twitter account
- Post tweets
- Follow people on Twitter
- Identify commonly used Twitter symbols and terms
- Understand about Twitter verification
- Learn how an account could get suspended
- Delete or deactivate your account
- Explore Twitter for Business

An Overview of Twitter

Twitter is a social media service launched by Twitter, Inc, California in March 2006.

It took some time to become popular, but soon grew to be one of the most popular social media platforms. By around 2012, more than 100 million users were active on Twitter each month. By 2018, the number rose to 330 million monthly users. Twitter enables users to communicate by posting quick, interactive messages called as tweets. The audience for your tweets may be friends, family, coworkers, or even complete strangers.

A tweet can contain text, photos, videos, and links. These tweets are posted to your profile and can be viewed by anyone who either *follows* you or just opens your profile. Tweets can also be searched via Twitter search through keywords.

These messages were originally restricted to 140 characters, but on November 7, 2017, the limit was doubled to 280 characters for all languages except Japanese, Korean, and Chinese.

You can create and post tweets only if you register (sign up). However, you can read tweets by others, even without registering.

Twitter Platform

Twitter is available for desktops through its Website interface, **http://twitter.com,** and for mobile phones through an app (such as Twitter for iPhone or iPad or Twitter for Android, and so on). For Apple devices, users can download the Twitter app from iTunes. For Android devices, users can download the app from Google Play Store.

Besides these native apps, third-party companies also offer Twitter clients such as TweetDeck, Plume, HootSuite, and others.

Twitter users can range from students, sportspersons, news journalists, government officials, to even Presidents of countries and heads of state. Celebrities use Twitter to promote themselves or their products. Regular people from various walks of life can use Twitter for a variety of purposes.

Twitter's Logo

Twitter now uses a signature bird logo called the *Twitter Bird*. Its first logo, though, was the word *Twitter* written in a fancy font. That logo was active from March 2006 to September 2010. This was then followed by a reworked version with *Larry the Bird* beside the old logo.

Finally, from June 2012 onwards, Twitter began using a new logo, a blue bird icon simply named as the Twitter Bird.

Figure 4.1: *Evolution of the Twitter Logo*

Getting Started with Twitter

Open the Twitter website on your desktop computer, install the Twitter client app on your phone/device, or install a third-party Twitter client. Once you have the Twitter screen open, click on **Login** or **Sign up**.

How-to: Create a Twitter Account

To begin with, you sign up to create an account.

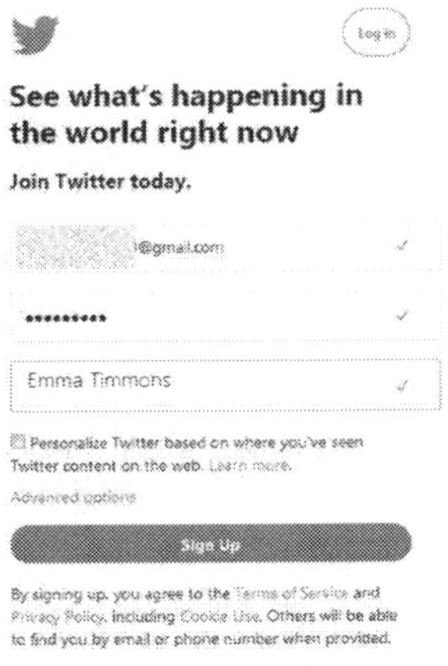

See what's happening in the world right now

Join Twitter today.

...@gmail.com

••••••••

Emma Timmons

Personalize Twitter based on where you've seen Twitter content on the web. Learn more.

Advanced options

Sign Up

By signing up, you agree to the Terms of Service and Privacy Policy, including Cookie Use. Others will be able to find you by email or phone number when provided.

Figure 4.2: *Signing Up*

After you enter your details and click Sign up, you will be prompted to choose a username. The username will appear in your profile and is called as your *handle*. Every handle, when in use, is prefixed with an @.

Choose a username.

Don't worry, you can always change it later.

Username

Figure 4.3: Choosing a Username

Thus, if you choose *emmatx2018* as your username, other Twitter users can *mention* your handle using *@emmatx2018*.

Next, Twitter will prompt you for your interests. Choose whatever areas of interests you are keen on.

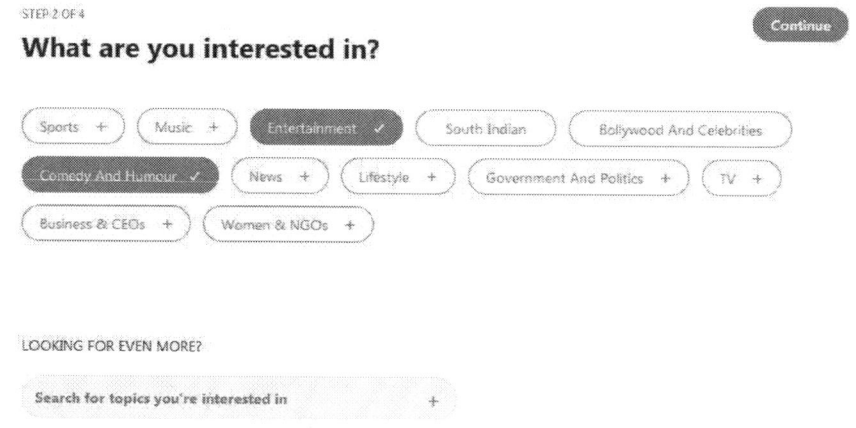

Figure 4.4: Choosing Interests

Then, click on **Continue**.

Based on your interests, Twitter will suggest whom to *follow*. To *follow* someone means that you have subscribed to their Twitter updates. Their posts will appear on your Twitter feed. If, instead, you wish to specifically follow some other accounts, you can enter the handle name.

How-to: Follow Twitter Users

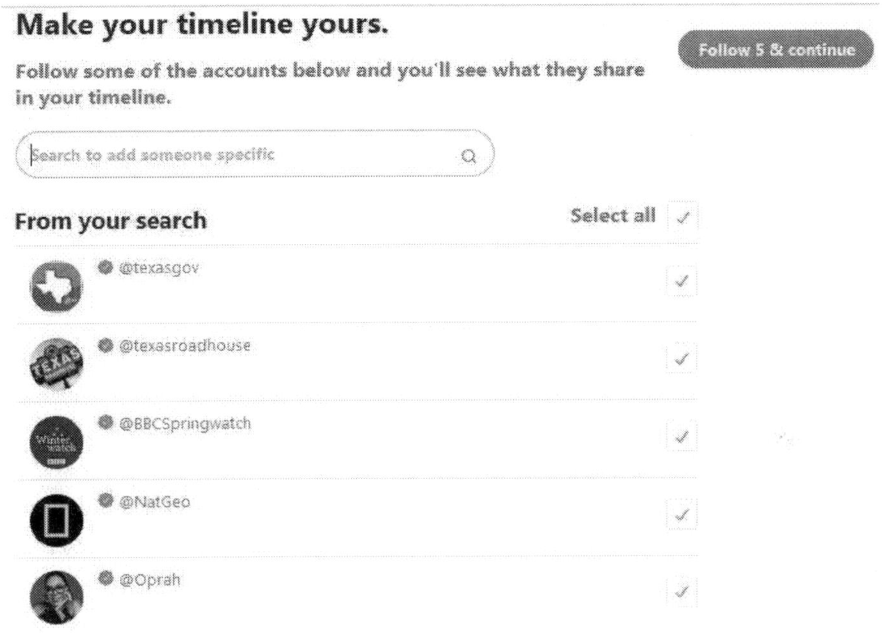

Make your timeline yours.

Follow some of the accounts below and you'll see what they share in your timeline.

Follow 5 & continue

Search to add someone specific 🔍

From your search   Select all ✓

⊘ @texasgov ✓

⊘ @texasroadhouse ✓

⊘ @BBCSpringwatch ✓

⊘ @NatGeo ✓

⊘ @Oprah ✓

Figure 4.5: Following Twitter Users

Click **Follow & continue** to proceed further. Your account will be successfully set up, and you will be directed to your timeline.

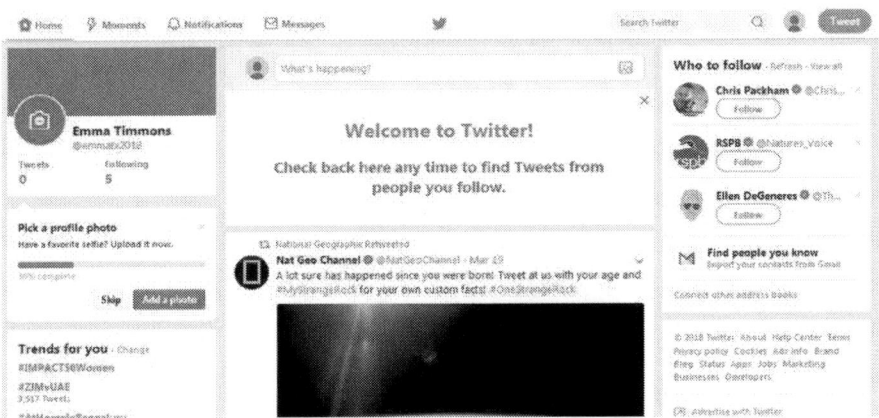

Figure 4.6: Twitter Timeline

As you can observe, there are various areas on your Twitter page.

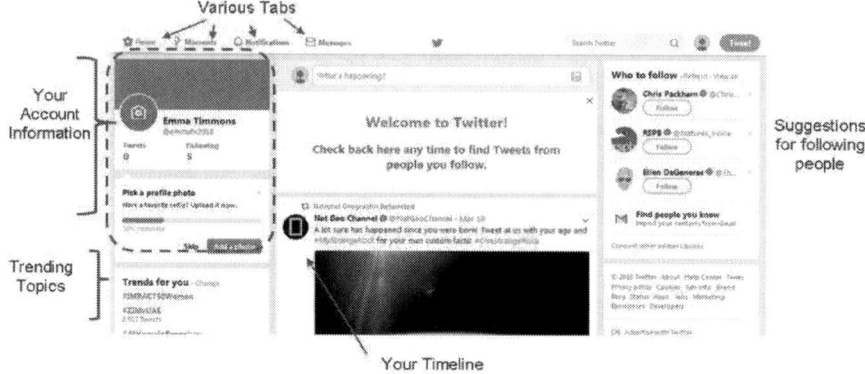

Figure 4.7: *Understanding the Twitter Page*

You can edit your display header photo and profile photo by clicking the blue area and camera icon respectively. You can upload pictures from your local computer as your header and profile photos.

For example, here we have edited the account information for Emma Timmons and set the display header photo and profile photo.

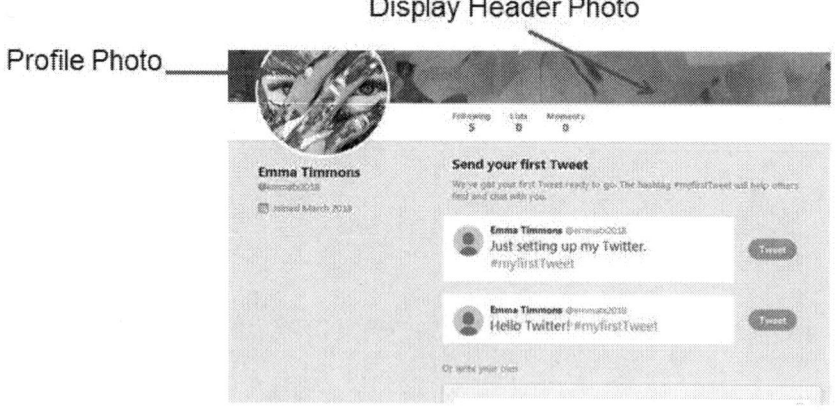

Figure 4.8: *Editing Your Profile*

What Can You Do on Twitter?

Once you are logged in, you can read tweets, *post* (compose and publish) tweets, share other's tweets with your followers (also called a retweet), and *follow* and *unfollow* people.

You can post pictures, video clips, and GIFs as part of tweets on Twitter.

 Twitter has an in-built option for GIFs. Click the **GIF** *button when composing a tweet to select any GIF image of your choice.*

You can also post emojis along with the text. A Twitter emoji is a specific series of letters immediately preceded by the # sign which autogenerates an icon on Twitter. Twitter now supports over 1100 emoji, including country flags, worldwide movements (such as #BlackLivesMatter), hand gestures, and smileys.

For example, just typing NBA automatically renders a special emoji created for **National Basketball Association (NBA),** men's premier professional basketball league in North America.

 *Remember, if you make a mistake, there's no way to edit a tweet after you have posted it. The only option is to delete the tweet and re-post the correct version.*

Followers versus Following

When you *follow* someone, any new message they post, will appear on your Twitter timeline (also called TL for short).

 *When you follow a large number of people, the tweets of all those people will appear on your feed, therefore you may not be shown every tweet of the people you follow. A workaround for this is to visit the timeline of the people whose tweets you don't want to miss out and then scroll through their tweets. For example, to view all the recent tweets by @TheFilmStage, you can just head to their Twitter page and read the tweets one by one.*

Notifications

The people whom you follow, will be notified when you begin following them, unless they have explicitly turned notifications off.

Likewise, people can *follow* you. This means that they subscribe to your Twitter updates. Any new tweet you post, will be visible to them on their TL.

Whenever someone starts to follow you, Twitter sends you a notification to indicate the same.

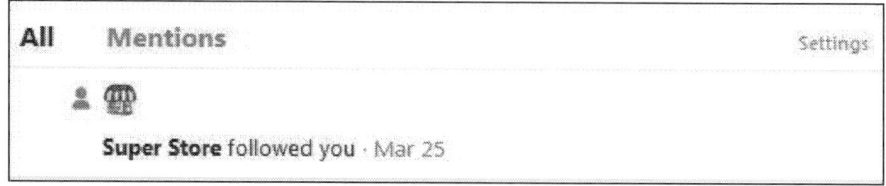

Figure 4.9: Twitter Notification

If you don't want to be notified of every new follower, you can configure your notifications in your settings. Settings are different for Twitter on Web, and Twitter mobile app.

Following are some notification settings for Twitter on Web.

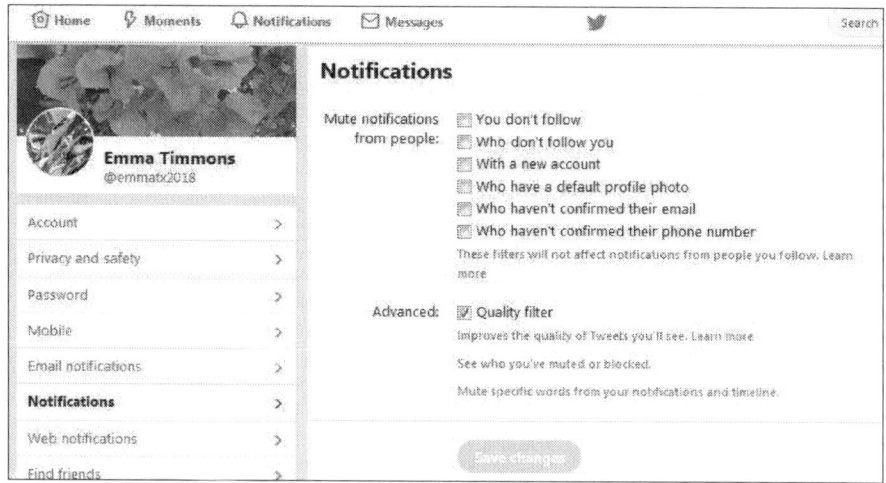

Figure 4.10: Configuring Notification Settings

Protecting Your Account

Tweets are public by default and if someone searches for any keyword in your Tweet, they can see that message. For example, suppose you wrote a tweet a week ago – "I love pineapple pizza" and someone searches for "pineapple pizza", then your tweet will show up in the results.

To secure your account and tweets from such access, you can protect your account so that only approved persons can get access to your tweets.

Twitter Symbols and Terms

Symbol	What It Means
Timeline	A timeline that appears on your Twitter home page displays a stream of Tweets from accounts that you follow. It is often abbreviated to TL.
Twitter Bio	Your bio or profile description is a short (up to 160 characters) personal description that appears in your profile. You can use it to tell people about yourself.
# (hashtag)	A hashtag is a word or phrase following the # symbol. Clicking a hashtag will display tweets from all over the world containing that same keyword or topic. For example,#photooftheday is a hashtag to curate daily amazing photographs from everywhere.
@	The @ sign is used to refer usernames in tweets. For example, to write a tweet to or reply to Emma Timmons, you can use @ emmatx2018, like Hi there @ emmatx2018
Reply	When you respond to another person's Tweet, it is called a reply. A reply is, by default, public, which means anyone can see the reply, not just the recipient.
Direct Message	A **Direct Message (DM)** is a private message and can only be seen by the sender and intended recipients. Direct Messages can be sent to one person or several persons at a time by adding them in a DM group.

Symbol	What It Means
Geolocation, Geotagging	Adding a location to your Tweet, also called a geolocation or geotag, short for geography tag, informs people who see your Tweet where you were, when you posted that Tweet.
Bookmark	This is a new feature introduced in February 2018. It allows users to save tweets privately, to be viewed later. Sort of like how you save bookmarks in your browser. You can also remove saved bookmarks when they are no longer needed.
Like	Earlier, the Like icon (heart icon) had two purposes: first, to favorite or bookmark a tweet for later reading and second, to indicate that you appreciate the tweet. Now with the introduction of Bookmarks, the Like (heart) icon serves only one purpose, to indicate that, you *like* or *appreciate* the tweet. When others *like* your tweet, you will be notified of it by default, unless you turn it off under your notification settings.
Mute	Mute here means to *silence*. You can mute accounts; mute words, phrases, usernames and hashtags from your notifications; and mute Direct Message notifications.
Block	This is a feature that helps you in restricting specific accounts from contacting you or interacting with you, preventing your tweets appear in their personal timeline of tweets. Their tweets won't be visible to you either.

Symbol	What It Means
Pin	Pinning a tweet means keeping a tweet fixed on your profile, so that when others visit your profile, it is the first tweet they see.
Trends	A Trend is a topic or hashtag determined through algorithms to be one of the most popular on Twitter at that instant. Trending topics usually show up on the left pane of desktop Twitter and under Search if viewed on a Twitter mobile client.
Moment	Moments are curated stories showcasing the best of what's happening on Twitter. You cannot add your Tweets to another person's Moment. Only the Moment author can decide which Tweets to include in the Moment.

Table 4.1

Twitter Verification

Verification is a process through which a Twitter account receives a blue check icon to indicate that the creator of the Tweets is a *verified* and genuine source. Verification gives users perks such as status, clout, freebies from brands, and so on. Verified users can also view replies or mentions from only other verified accounts.

Celebrities, famous personalities from various domains, including politics, sports, entertainment, business, and so on often have verified accounts.

Some examples of famous verified accounts include *@justinbieber* (106 million followers), *@YouTube* (71.9 million followers), *@ElonMusk* (21.5 million followers), and The Ellen Show (77.8 million followers).

Figure 4.11: Verified Accounts

Account Suspension

Twitter often suspends accounts that violate Twitter Rules. Accounts that spam, abuse, or threaten people are commonly suspended.

Suspension may be temporary or, in some cases, permanent.

 *To know more about suspensions, visit this link:*

https://help.twitter.com/en/managing-your-account/ suspended-twitter-accounts

Deactivating or Deleting Your Account

Deactivation is the first step before deleting your account. It puts your account in a queue for deletion from Twitter. However, if you change your mind within 30 days, you can get back your account by reactivating it.

 *Deactivation cannot be done via an app must be done by accessing twitter.com on the Web.*

To deactivate your account, login and go to the **Settings and privacy** option from the drop-down menu under your profile icon. Click **Deactivate your account** at the bottom of the page. Read the information shown and then, click **Deactivate** your @username.

Enter your password, and confirm that your account should be deactivated.

Twitter Advertising

For businesses, Twitter offers paid advertising and targeted ad campaigns. They can create customized campaigns around their business objectives, audiences, and budget. They can also track growth of their follower base and explore how users are engaging with every tweet.

Businesses can also leverage the Twitter Developer platform using which they can build products with Twitter data, create Twitter advertising campaigns, and incorporate Twitter into their products. Twitter's data products, Ads API, and publisher tools can be used to do this.

These days, a lot of brands including movie franchises and shows have their own Twitter handle for publicity and promotion. *@starwars* and *@Avengers* are popular examples.

To learn more about Twitter Ads, visit:

https://business.twitter.com/

https://business.twitter.com/en/solutions/twitter-ads.html

https://business.twitter.com/en/help/troubleshooting/how-twitter-ads-work.html

Summary

- Twitter is a social media service that allows you to post text, images, videos, and more in the form of tweets.
- Twitter is available for desktop as well as for mobile phones.
- The Twitter logo is a blue bird icon, called the *TwitterBird*.
- To *follow* someone means that you have subscribed to their Twitter updates. Their posts will appear on your Twitter feed.
- If, instead, you wish to specifically follow some other accounts, you can enter the handle name.
- Verified accounts on Twitter have a blue check icon and are eligible for special features.
- Twitter can suspend your account if you are found to be violating their rules. You can delete your account by first deactivating it which places your account in a queue for

30 days. If you change your mind within 30 days, you can reactivate your account.

- Twitter offers paid advertising and targeted ad campaigns for businesses.

Chapter 4 Quiz

1. You can create and post tweets only if you register (sign up) on Twitter. [True/False]

2. Display header photo and profile photo are the same thing and show the same content. [True/False]

3. Notification settings are different for Twitter on Web and Twitter mobile app. [True/False]

4. _____ is a new feature introduced in February 2018 which allows users to save tweets privately so that they can be viewed later.

5. On Twitter, you can show appreciation for someone's tweet by clicking the _____ button/icon.

CHAPTER 5
Facebook

In this chapter, we look at one of the most popular social media platforms - *Facebook*.

Objectives

By the end of this chapter, you will be able to:

- Understand the Facebook platform
- Identify key features of Facebook
- Sign Up for a Facebook account
- Create a Facebook Timeline
- Add friends, like pages, share photos, and post status updates
- Use Facebook on Mobile
- Delete or deactivate your account

Introduction to Facebook

As of today, nearly everyone is on Facebook or FB as it's called popularly. Even the local neighborhood *paan-walla* could be having his own FB account. Facebook is an American social media and social networking service company. It was founded in 2004 by a group of Harvard College students, namely, Mark Zuckerberg, Eduardo Saverin, Andrew McCollum, Dustin Moskovitz, and Chris Hughes. The Website *Facebook.com* was launched in 2005.

The founders initially limited membership to the site exclusively to Harvard students. Soon, they expanded it to higher education institutions in the Boston area, the Ivy League schools, and Stanford University. Facebook gradually added support for students at various other universities, and eventually to high school students. In 2007, Facebook mobile was launched.

Facebook got its name from the *face book directories* that are often given to American university students.

Features of Facebook

Facebook was the first social network to surpass 1 billion registered accounts and currently sits at 2.2 billion monthly active users.

Using Facebook, you can:
- Connect with friends
- Search for friends
- Plan for events and engagements
- Invite people to events and engagements
- Create and promote a business page
- Share photos
- Share your thoughts, news snippets, and status updates

Activities on Facebook

Friending and Unfriending

Friending someone is the act of sending another user a friend request on Facebook. When you send someone a friend request and they accept it, or someone sends you a friend request and you accept it, the two of you become Facebook friends.

In place of accepting the request, a user can also decline the friend request or hide it using the *Not Now* feature.

When you delete a friend request, the request is removed, but the sender will not be able to resend it in the future. On the other hand, the Not Now feature hides the request but does not delete it, thus permitting you (receiver) to revisit and possibly accept the request later.

Facebook has set a limit of 5000 for connections, which is not just for friends but for connections in general. A person can have a maximum of 5,000 connections on Facebook, including both friends and pages. A Facebook Page is a public profile specifically created for a business or brand. Celebrities, causes, and other organizations too make use of the Facebook page feature.

People who choose to *like* a Facebook page become fans of the page, not a *friend*. Thus, an organization or a celebrity will attract likes and fans.

It is also possible to remove a user from one's friends, which is referred to as unfriending by Facebook.

Creating and Updating a Timeline

Earlier Facebook had a feature called Wall as well as Profile, which are now replaced by Timeline. In other words, Timeline is a section of your Facebook account. It shows the story of your life in a visual, scrolling, reverse-chronologically ordered timeline.

A Timeline shows status updates, photos, friendships, as well as your background information such as education, job history, marital status changes, and other information that are added in your profile.

You don't have to make your relationship status public if you don't feel like it.

Timeline or profile page is where other people will go to look for your information on Facebook. Similarly, you can go to your friends' Timeline to check them out.

Viewing your stream

When you login to Facebook, you will be shown a *stream* of information which are basically posted or shared by your friends.

Sharing a post or link

The link you shared will appear on the feed with a message to the viewers, notifying them that you have shared the link. Refer to *Figure 5.1.*

Figure 5.1: Example of a Shared Link

Liking

The *Like* button is one of the simplest Facebook features and acts like an approval or appreciation. Your friends can click *Like* on your posts or shares and you can click Like on their posts and shares.

Adding Reactions and Comments

Reactions allow users to long-press on Like button for an option to use one of five pre-defined emotions, including *Love, Haha, Wow, Sad,* or *Angry*. Reactions were also extended to comments in 2017.

Now, let's use these features hands-on.

How-to: Create a Facebook Account

1. First, open the Facebook Website. You will see a page like *Figure 5.2*.

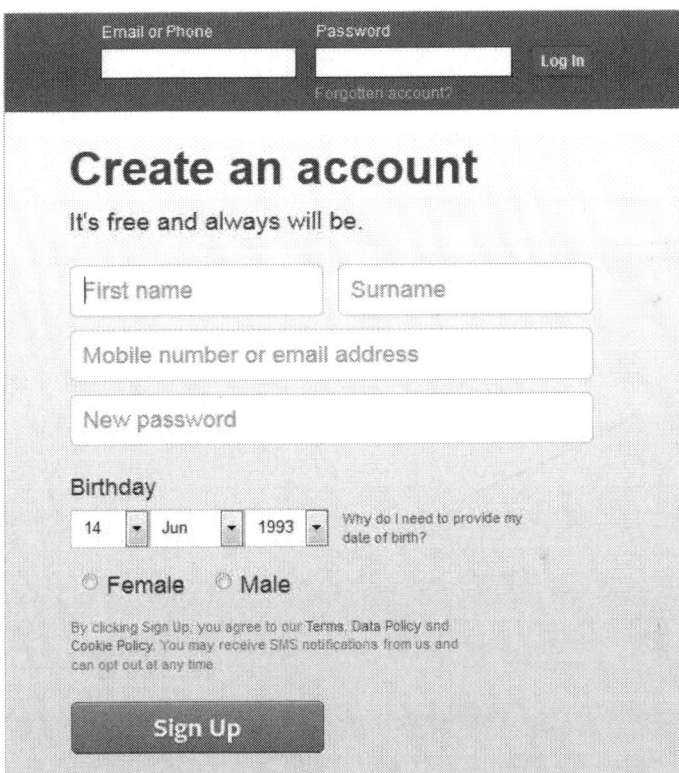

Figure 5.2: *Creating a Facebook Account*

2. Type in all the requisite details and click on **Sign Up** button.

3. You will be prompted to create your profile page, upload a profile photo and create a cover photo.

How-to: Create a Facebook Profile

1. Click on **Edit Profile** to edit your profile. Refer to *Figure 5.3* and *5.4.*

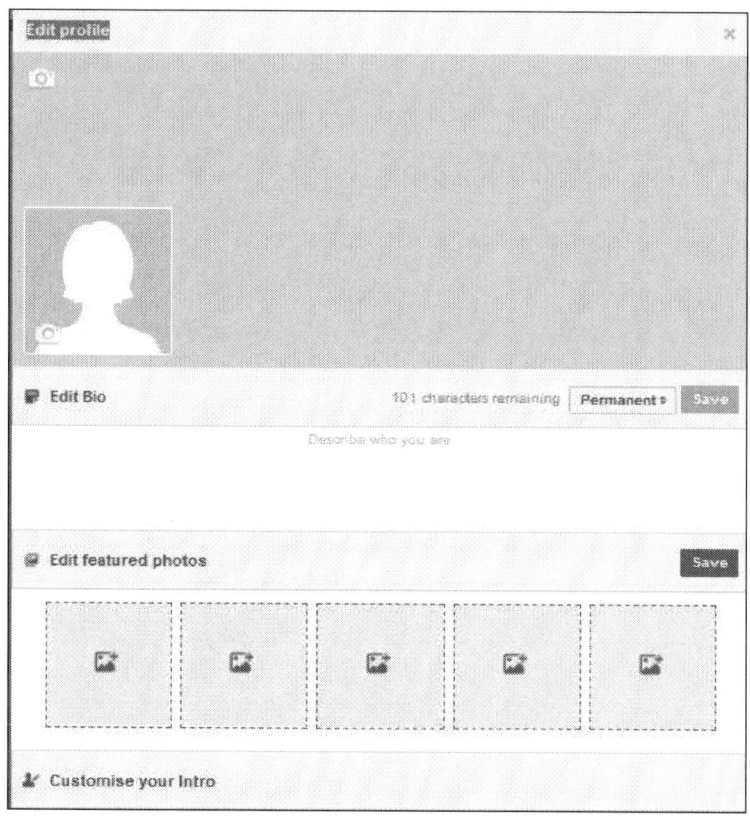

Figure 5.3: Editing Profile

Figure 5.4: Editing Profile (Continued)

2. Add personal information such as your birthday, anniversary, job details, and more on your profile.

How-to: Explore Facebook Features

1. Once your profile is ready, connect with family, friends, and others by sending them a *friend request*. Facebook may prompt you with suggestions whom to add. Refer to *Figure 5.5*.

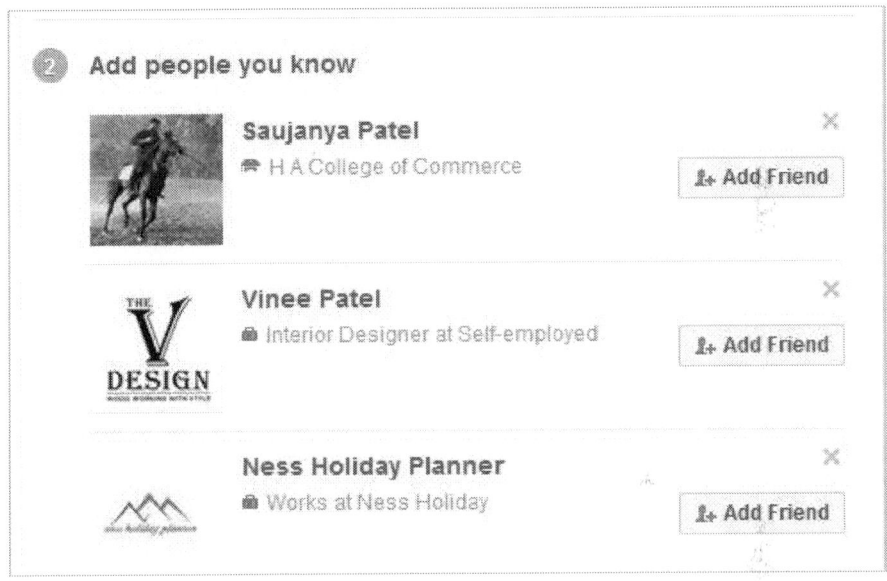

Figure 5.5: Adding Friends

2. You can then configure your privacy settings and decide who gets to see what. Refer to *Figure 5.6*.

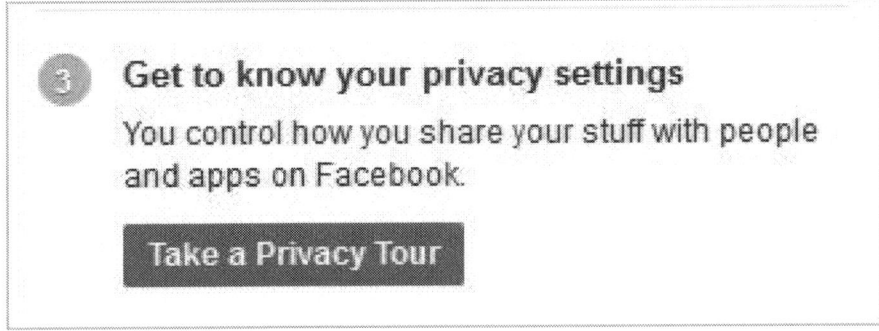

Figure 5.6: Configuring Privacy Settings - Tour

1. If you click on **Take a Privacy Tour,** a four-step wizard as shown in *Figure 5.7* will take through a quick tour of the various privacy settings you can configure.

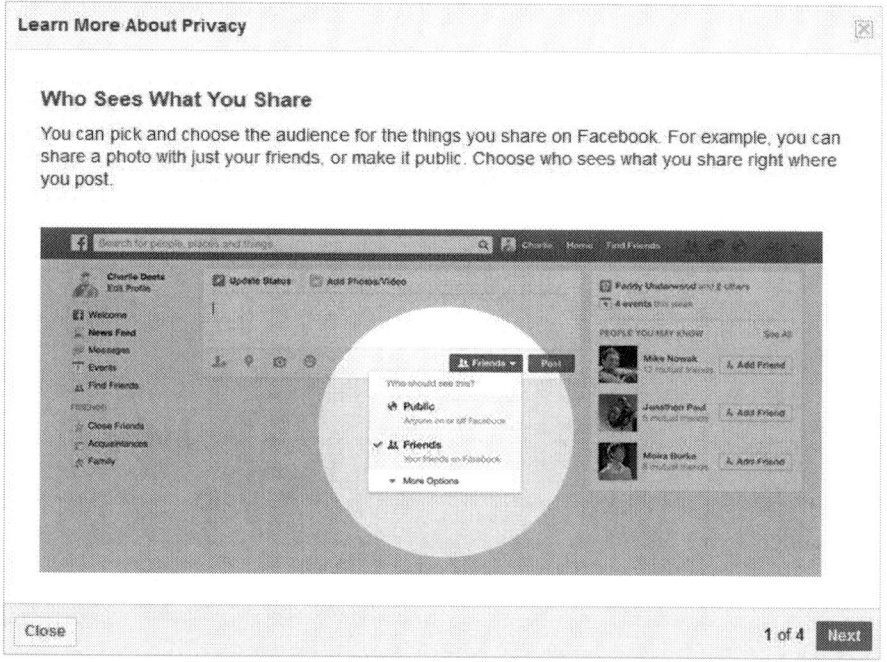

Figure 5.7: Configuring Privacy Settings

The icons on the top right corner as shown in *Figure 5.8* help you manage friend requests, messages, notifications, and so on.

Figure 5.8: Icons on the Main Page

The panel on the left as shown in Figure 5.9 shows various options that you can use on Facebook.

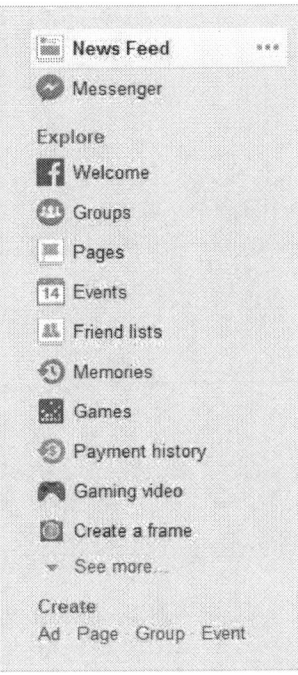

Figure 5.9: Options on the Left Panel

2. You can put up a status update or a post comprising text, photos, and/or videos. Refer to *Figure 5.10.*

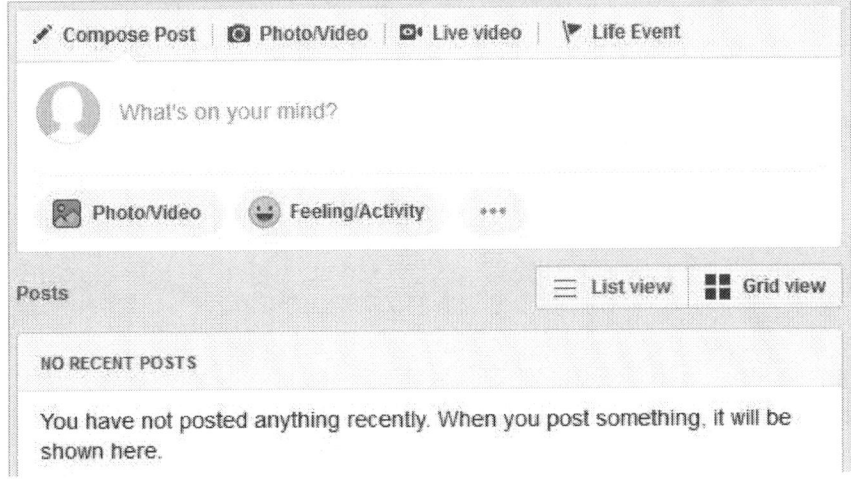

Figure 5.10: Status Update

3. By using the **Feeling/Activity** button, you can add a *feeling* or activity to your post. Refer to *Figure 5.11*.

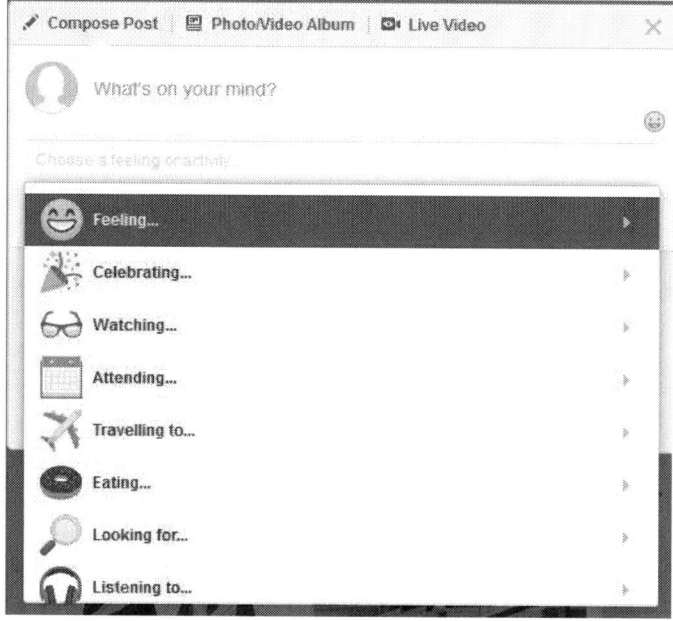

Figure 5.11: *Feeling/Activity Button*

4. You can like, share, or comments on others' posts. Refer to the buttons at the bottom of *Figure 5.12*.

Figure 5.12: *Buttons below the Post*

TIPS:

Check out these links to make the most from Facebook.

https://www.forbes.com/sites/ amitchowdhry/2013/11/19/facebook-privacy-tips/#4f7c0f121a46

https://www.hongkiat.com/blog/most-wanted-facebook-tips-and-tricks/http://www.digitalspy. com/tech/internet/feature/a822986/secret-facebook-features-tips-tricks/https://www.pcmag.com/ feature/324797/28-hidden-facebook-features-only-power-users-know

Facebook Messenger

Facebook messenger is a mobile messaging app, that is a companion to the Facebook site. Formerly called as Facebook Chat, the mobile app enables users to send instant messages and exchange photos, videos, audio, and files, as well as react to other users' messages and interact with bots. Users can also make voice and video calls.

Refer to *Figure 5.13* to see how Facebook Messenger looks like.

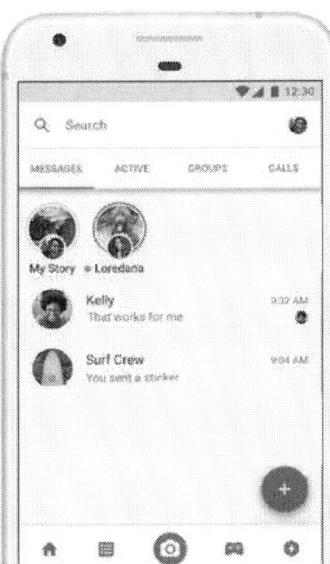

Figure 5.13: Facebook Messenger

Based on your device (Android or iPhone/iPad), install the app from the respective app store.

To send a message through Facebook messenger on Android:

1. From **Home**, tap the ▣ icon in the bottom right.

2. Type or click a contact's name.

3. Type a message in the text box at the bottom.

4. Tap ➤ icon to send.

Open any conversation, then tap any of these options:

- Take and send new photos or videos
- Send photos or videos
- Record a voice message
- Send stickers, GIFs or emoji

You can delete messages, conversations and photos from your inbox. You can sync your Contacts on your phone with your messenger app. Besides these tasks, you can also do a lot more through Facebook messenger.

Tips: Check out some tips and tricks for the app here: **https://www.techytab.com/2017/06/facebook-messenger-tricks-tips-secrets-2018.html**

https://www.guidingtech.com/top-facebook-messenger-tips-android-2018/

Facebook for Business

The reach of Facebook spreads across more than 2 billion active users. This makes Facebook an economical and effective way to market your business. You can target a specific audience through paid campaigns. Since Facebook has a lot of information about its users, it can use this to your advantage when you opt for Facebook marketing.

You begin by visiting **https://www.facebook.com/pages/creation/**as shown in *Figure 5.14* and then selecting the appropriate option.

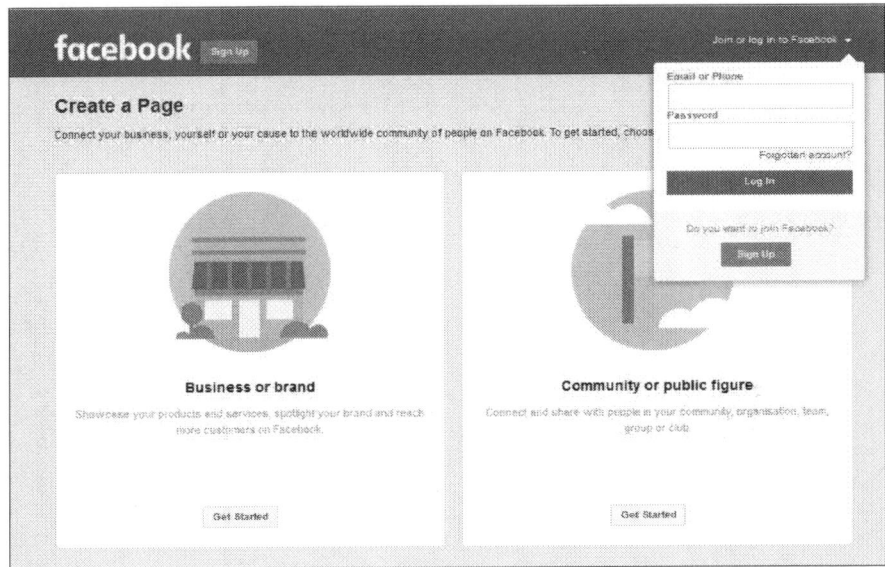

Figure 5.14: Facebook Pages

Create a Facebook brand page for your business by selecting the button **Get Started** on the left. Supply basic general information such as name, username, and business category, and contact information. Then, include details about your business, such as your Website, social accounts, default, and cover photos, *about* section, hours, and location.

You can add a **call-to-action** button to the top of your page, to encourage visitors to interact. Call-to-actions for customers can include get in *touch, shop now, download an app,* and so on.

On the left of your page, you can add a link for **customer reviews.** Customers can rate your business/services and write reviews. Reviews and ratings will show up at the top of your page and can help grow your business.

The **messages** option at the top of your page redirects to an inbox with messages from your customers/audience. It is not much different from the chat feature on Facebook, but it allows you to respond as your business.

Facebook Insights is a free analytics tool provided by Facebook. It shows data on actions taken, page views, the number of people you have reached, the number of post engagements, and more. Such results can help build a robust social media campaign.

Facebook Publishing Tools allow you to schedule posts to go live in the future. You can also create videos, advertise your business, promote an event, and post job applications here.

Facebook also provides a **polling** feature that allows you to get your followers' opinions.

If you selected **Get Started** on the right, on the page shown in *Figure 5.14*, you will create a community page. A **community page** allows customers to add posts, photos, and videos.

Controversy

In 2017-18, Facebook has had several controversies, including data breach of 87 million users without their consent, enabling creation of fake Russian paid accounts, and more.

Summary

- Facebook is a social networking platform that helps people connect with one another.
- Users can sign up and create a profile on Facebook.
- When a user connects to a person through Facebook, it is called as 'friending'.
- Users can upload text, photos, and videos to their daily feed.
- Users can like, share or comment on other's posts.
- Facebook messenger is a mobile app that enables people to send instant messages and exchange photos, videos, audio, and files, as well as react to other users' messages and interact with bots.

Chapter 5 Quiz

1. You can have up to 6000 connections on Facebook. [True/False]

2. You can add your personal information such as your marital status, wedding anniversary, and job history in your Facebook profile. [True/False]

3. It is not possible to sync your mobile address book with Facebook. [True/False]

4. You can add a feeling or activity to your Facebook post. [True/False]

5. Facebook Messenger app is available only for Android phones. [True/False]

CHAPTER 6
WhatsApp

In this chapter, we shall explore the popular messaging application, WhatsApp.

Objectives

By the end of this chapter, you will be able to:

- Understand the basics of WhatsApp platform
- Identify key features of WhatsApp
- Understand how to install WhatsApp on mobile and desktop
- Use WhatsApp to send voice messages, photos, videos, and more
- Conduct voice and video calls
- Explore WhatsApp for Business

An Overview of WhatsApp

WhatsApp is a messaging application. It was created in 2009 at WhatsApp Inc which was founded by Brian Acton and Jan Koum, ex-employees of Yahoo!. Shortly thereafter, the app was officially launched for the iOS App Store and then, targeted for release, for all major operating systems, including Android and Blackberry.

With minimal marketing, the application went on to become the most popular messaging platform, out-performing its competitors. It was acquired by Facebook in February 2014.

Initially, for a few years, users could only communicate with other users individually or in groups of individual users. In January 2018, WhatsApp launched WhatsApp Business for small businesses to facilitate customer service.

WhatsApp's reach has extended far and wide, including countries such as India, Africa, Brazil, Germany, United Kingdom, and France. Of these, India and South Africa are top markets.

Around 60 languages are supported by WhatsApp.

Table 6.1 shows WhatsApp's growth in recent years.

Year	Number of Monthly Active Users Worldwide
2014	600 Million
2015	700 Million
2017	1.3 Billion
2018	1.5 Billion

Table 6.1

Key Features of WhatsApp
Allows you to Send Texts

Using WhatsApp, you can send messages over your phone's Internet connection to friends, and family members, and others. The charges for this will depend on your data provider.

Enables participation in group chats

Group chats allow you to send and receive messages as a group. Be it workplace chats with coworkers or family gupshups or just hanging out online with friends, this feature is perfect for all of those. A group can have any number of people up to a maximum of 256. You can share photos, videos, and documents with the entire group at once. The person who manages the group is called an *admin*. The group admin has special privileges and can add or remove people to/from the group. Other members of the group can perform tasks such as naming the group, muting, or customizing notifications, and more.

Enables sharing of documents and reports

In 2016, WhatsApp added a new feature: document sharing. Users can easily send PDFs, documents, spreadsheets, slideshows, and more of up to 100 MB.

Enables you to record and send voice messages

You can record and send a Voice Message through WhatsApp.

Enables you to stay safe with end-to-end encryption

WhatsApp has end-to-end encryption for messages which means that only you and the recipient can read or listen to them. No one else, not even WhatsApp, can view your messages.

Allows you to make Voice and Video Calls via WhatsApp

WhatsApp Voice calls enable you to talk to your friends and family for free (data charges apply). This applies even internationally. You can also make video calls. These calls (voice and video) use your phone's Internet connection and standard data charges will apply.

Enables you to share photos and videos

Through WhatsApp, you can send photos and videos instantly. There's a built-in camera using which you can even capture and send.

Using WhatsApp Web

Besides the mobile app, WhatsApp offers a desktop app and a Web-based version. Thanks to this, you can use WhatsApp on your computer as well through the desktop app and WhatsApp Web. You can sync chats with your computer so that you can chat any time anywhere on whichever device is most convenient for you.

How-to: Install and Configure WhatsApp

1. Depending on your smartphone OS (Android, iOS, or BlackBerry), you can go to the respective app store to find the WhatsApp app and download it to your phone.

2. To sign up, you need to provide your phone number. You will then receive an authentication code (One-time Password or OTP) on your phone.

3. Once you type in the OTP, you can edit sections of your profile, such as your About Message and Display Picture. This can be done when setting up WhatsApp for the first time as well as any time later. Say, you want to change your Display Picture every week. You can do that by all means!

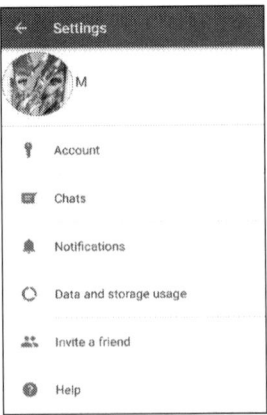

Figure 6.1: Settings

4. You can configure various **Settings** options, such as Font size for chats, notifications, and more.

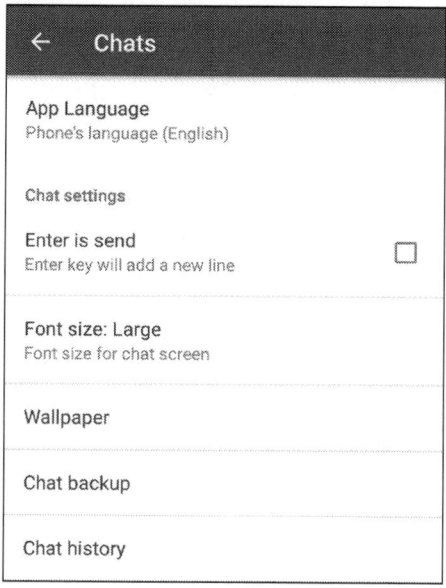

Figure 6.2: Chat Settings

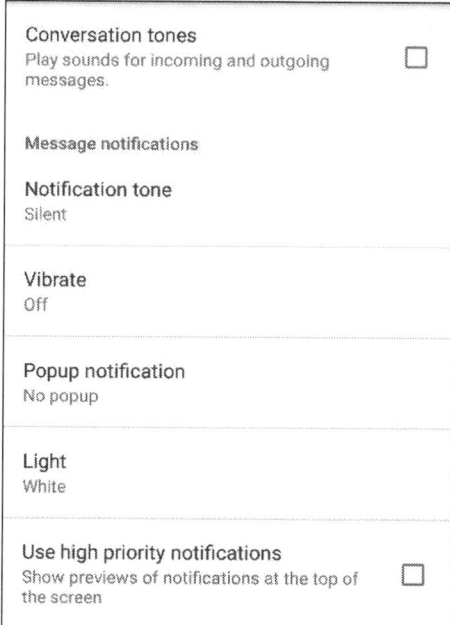

Figure 6.3: Sound and Notifications

Install WhatsApp on your computer

Visit **https://www.whatsapp.com/download** or Apple App Store to download and install the desktop version on your computer.

Supported operating systems include Windows 8 (or later) or Mac OSX 10.9 (or newer) versions. Older versions of these OS will not support the software.

Use WhatsApp Web on browser

The WhatsApp Web client version that can run directly on your browser (such as Chrome, Firefox, or others) is called as **WhatsApp Web**. This does not require any local installation.

To launch WhatsApp Web,

1. Open the URL **https://web.whatsapp.com** in your desktop browser.
2. Open the WhatsApp app on your phone.
3. Scan the WhatsApp QR code displayed on the browser screen with your phone.
4. Upon successful scanning, you can start using it. Note that data charges are not reduced because you use it on the Web. Standard data charges will continue to apply.

How-to: Add Contacts to Your WhatsApp

WhatsApp has access to your phone's address book and retrieves your contacts' phone numbers into the app automatically. When you click on **Refresh** button in WhatsApp, you can see all your contacts who are already available on WhatsApp. You can also invite friends who are not yet on WhatsApp.

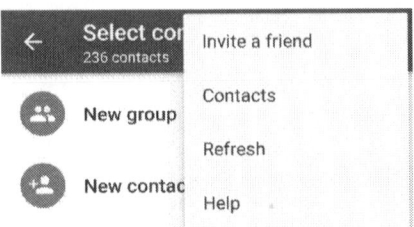

Figure 6.4: Adding Contacts

Receiving messages from unknown numbers

It may happen that while on WhatsApp, you may see a message sent to you from someone whose number you do not recognize. This number may not be saved in your address book. You can either save their contact information by tapping **Add to contacts** (exercise caution while doing this though) or report the message as spam.

How-to: Send Messages in WhatsApp

1. Tap on a contact in your WhatsApp list. A chat window opens. At the bottom of the window, you will see some icons/ symbols.

    Refer to the highlighted areas in Figure 6.5.

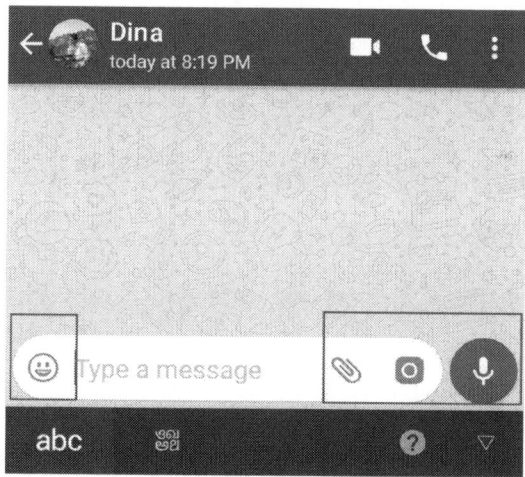

Figure 6.5: Chat Window

2. Type a text message, tap the symbol to send an attachment, or tap the symbol to click a picture or video using WhatsApp.

3. Use the first icon to send emojis in your text message.

4. Use the last icon to send a voice note via WhatsApp.

How-to: Make Calls in WhatsApp

1. Tap/click on a contact in your WhatsApp list. A chat window opens.

2. At the top, you will see three symbols. One is for making voice calls and the other is for making video calls. Refer to *Figure 6.6*.

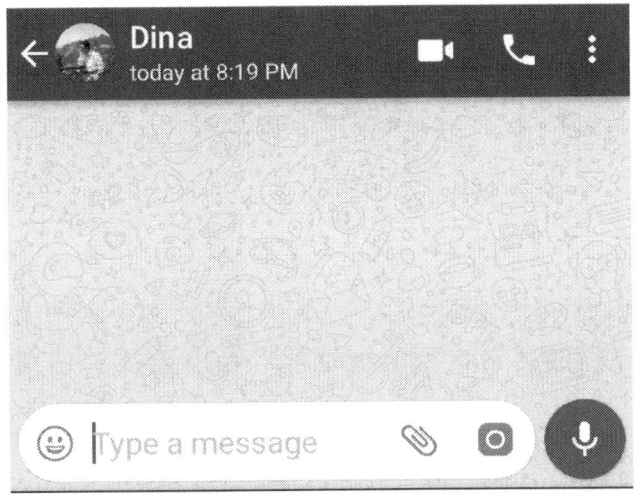

Figure 6.6: *Call Options in WhatsApp*

How-to: Use other options in the WhatsApp chat window

1. Tap the three dots on the right corner of the chat window to view the other options available.

2. You can block the contact, mute any notifications from the contact, view the contact's details such as number, status message, and soon.

How-to: Format messages in WhatsApp

You can also format text inside your chat messages by selecting the text and then applying one or more of the formats shown in *Table 6.2*.

Style	Description	Technique
Italic	*Italicize* your message	Place an underscore on both sides of the text: _text_
Bold	Apply **bold** format to your message	Place an asterisk on both sides of the text: *text*
~~Strikethrough~~	Apply ~~strikethrough~~ to your message	Place a tilde on both sides of the text: ~text~

Table 6.2

How-to: Work with the groups feature in WhatsApp

WhatsApp Groups facilitate people to connect and communicate as a group.

You can connect with family members, friends, or co-workers across the world.

Schools may have WhatsApp groups of parents. Students can form groups for study sessions.

- **Group description:** A short description found under group info, using which you can specify the purpose, guidelines, or topics for the group. When a new member joins the group, he/she can view the description at the top of the chat. Existing members can also view the description anytime.

- **Admin controls:** Group settings also include a control, using which, admins can limit who can change the group's subject, icon, and description.

Creating Groups

To create a new group, click the corner of the WhatsApp window, then tap **New Group**. Provide a name for the group.

Add members to the group from your WhatsApp contact list.

How-to: Delete media and chat history in WhatsApp

Delete WhatsApp media such as photos, GIFs, and videos from time to time, to clear storage space.

Clear chat history from each chat window, regardless of whether it's an individual chat or group chat. Go to **More Options** on the chat and then select **Clear Chat**.

How-to: Backup your WhatsApp chats

Backup your chat data on Google Drive periodically. You can automate this process or choose to take backup manually.

WhatsApp for Business

WhatsApp Business is a free Android-based app, intended for small business owners. Businesses can use tools to automate, sort, and quickly respond to messages and thus, have improved communication with customers. They can create a business profile with address, business description, email address, and website. They can also get significant metrics such as how many of their messages were successfully sent, delivered, and read.

Tips and Tricks

http://www.digitalspy.com/tech/apps/feature/ a780553/15-whatsapp-tips-and-tricks-to-turn-you- into-a-messaging-master/

https://www.hongkiat.com/blog/whatsapp-tips- tricks/

https://www.stuff.tv/features/33-secret-whatsapp- tricks-you-probably-didnt-know-about

Summary

- WhatsApp is a messaging application, using which you can send text, documents, photos, and videos, and make voice and video calls.
- WhatsApp is now owned by Facebook.
- Besides the mobile app, WhatsApp offers a desktop app and a Web-based version.
- WhatsApp also has a business version called WhatsApp for Business.

Chapter 6 Quiz

1. How many languages are supported by WhatsApp?
   A. Around 60
   B. 80
   C. Around 50
   D. 25

2. Now, using WhatsApp, users can easily send PDFs, documents, spreadsheets, slideshows, and more of up to
   _____.

3. WhatsApp has access to your phone's address book and retrieves your contacts' phone numbers into the app automatically. [True/False]

CHAPTER 7
Instagram

In this chapter, we look at another popular platform in the social media universe - *Instagram.*

▪ Objectives ▪────────────────────

By the end of this chapter, you will be able to:

- Identify key features of Instagram
- Sign Up for an Instagram account
- Follow people on Instagram
- Create and share an Instagram post
- Create and share an Instagram story
- Explore IGTV
- Delete or deactivate your account

Introduction to Instagram

Instagram is a social media platform primarily designed for photo-sharing. Using Instagram, you can apply filters to your photos and videos, and make them stand out. With Instagram, you can capture and share memorable moments. You can also follow others' posts (comprising photos, videos, and stories) on Instagram. As of today, it's available both as a mobile app (iOS and Android) and desktop based Website.

Figure 7.1: *Instagram Desktop Site*

Like Facebook and Twitter, anyone, be it a celebrity, a brand, a sportsperson, a royal person or an ordinary citizen, can have an account on Instagram.

Growth and Popularity

Instagram was founded in October 2010 by Kevin Systrom and Mike Krieger. Since then, it has grown a lot. The total number of monthly active Instagram users reached one billion in June 2018.

What you can do on Instagram (Features of Instagram)

Here are some of the things you can do on Instagram:

- Sign up and create an account of your own
- Add your bio

- Follow other people with similar interests
- Upload a picture from your phone
- Capture a live picture and upload on your account
- Add hashtags to your posts and stories
- Create a live story and share it
- Like and/or share others' posts
- Write comments on others' posts
- Save a post to a collection
- Share a post on another social media platform
- Tag people in your pictures
- Remove yourself from pictures you are tagged in
- Filter comments on your posts
- Turn comments off
- Turn off notifications
- Send people direct messages (DMs)

Photos and Videos

Instagram enables you to either click pictures/videos, or upload pictures/video from your device (such as phone, laptop, tablet, or computer) and then post it to your timeline, to be seen by others. For the former, you will need to grant Instagram access to your camera.

Profiles

A profile is a description that identifies you. It is up to you, what you wish to include in your profile. At minimum, a profile includes a username. It can also include your username, location, photo, a website, and a brief bio.

Profiles can also be made private, in which case, only people who want to follow you or view your timeline need to be approved by you. Only approved followers will be able to view or search your content.

Importance of using Hashtags

Hashtags help your posts to reach a broader audience. For example, if you added a hashtag #Spring to your picture of a flower, people across the world who click that hashtag can view your picture even if they do not follow you. The hashtag will enable your content to be easily discoverable by others. These days, people add multiple hashtags to their posts. However, if your profile is private, adding hashtags will not be of any use.

How-to - Create an Instagram account and Explore Instagram

1. Open the Instagram website or mobile app. You will be prompted with the Login/Sign up page.

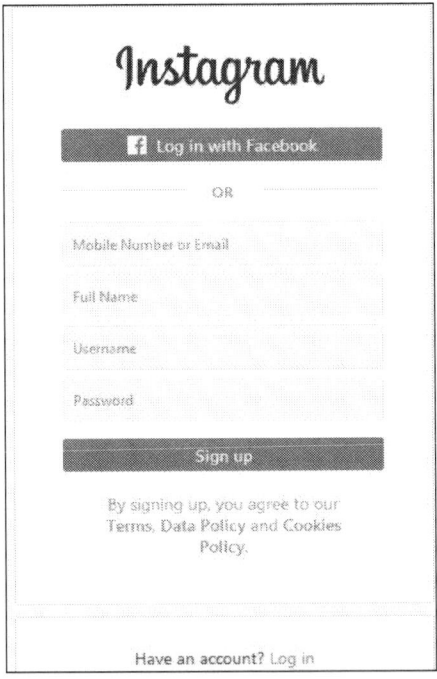

Figure 7.2: Instagram Login/Sign Up Page on Mobile

The first time you encounter this page, you will sign up by providing your credentials. Thereafter, just click on Login, and enter your username and password.

After you login the first time, you create your bio/profile and then follow other Instagram users based on your interests.

Since you are new to Instagram, you may need to first follow a few people. Choose whom to follow based on your interests.

For example, assume that you are interested to know about Elon Musk. You can open his profile page and click on **Follow** button, to follow his posts regularly.

Figure 7.3: *Instagram Profile Page*

Or consider that you are simply interested in science and want to follow a science related Instagram user.

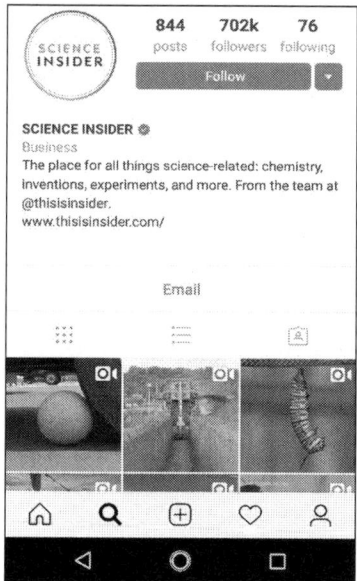

Figure 7.4: *Instagram Profile Page (Another Example)*

After you're logged in, you will be presented with your Instagram feed which is nothing but a series of posts by the people you follow. These days, Instagram also displays several advertisement posts in between the other posts.

Refer to *Figure 7.5* to see a sample post. A post usually consists of a picture or a set of pictures with a caption, optionally featuring tags and locations.

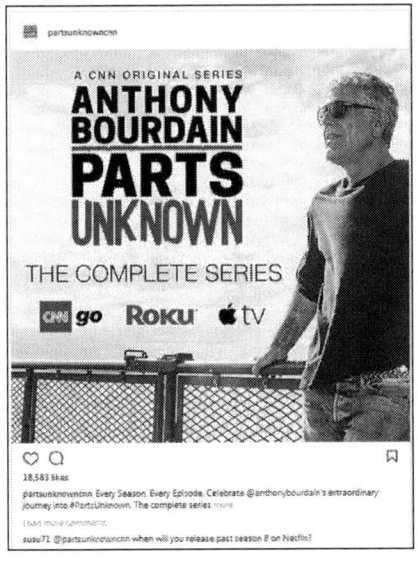

Figure 7.5: Instagram Post

Below each post, you can see the following four icons:

- **Heart,** to Like
- **Bubble,** to Comment
- **Arrow,** to Send a DM- Direct message
- **Save,** to save images to your account

Further below the post, underneath the like and comment icons, you can see the total number of likes, the post has received until that instance, and you can also see comments. By default, Instagram displays only one comment, and hides the rest. The message to get Instagram to show all the comments, differs between the website and the app.

On the website, Instagram displays **Load more comments** while on the app, it displays **View all x comments**, where x is the number of comments on that post.

Scroll down the feed on your app or the website to view more posts. Click the search icon on the top to search for posts based on usernames, hashtags, or locations.

Figure 7.6 shows a search made for the hashtag #kingfisher.

Figure 7.6: *Instagram Search Results*

Click on any of the posts shown to view it in expanded mode.

Figure 7.7: *Expanded Mode*

Click **Follow** to follow the user. On Instagram, there is no feature like a Friend Request. You can follow any account you like, as long as their profile is public. If an account profile is protected, it means that the user will receive a follow request from you and has to approve your request. Only if they approve it, you will be granted access to their pictures.

Click the *Heart* icon to like the picture. You can also double tap on a picture in the mobile app to *like* it. If the user who posted the picture has not turned their notifications off (you will learn more on this shortly later), they will receive a notification that you have *liked* their picture. Likewise, if someone else likes your post and you haven't turned your notifications off, you will receive a notification that someone liked your picture. It is not necessary to follow someone in order to *like* their picture.

Click the **bubble** icon to add a comment. Comments act like feedback. You can write appreciative comments or just observations. Sometimes, you can even write comments on your post to elaborate a description.

Configuring Settings

On your account page, at the top corner, you will see three vertical dots. Click this to bring up the Settings screen.

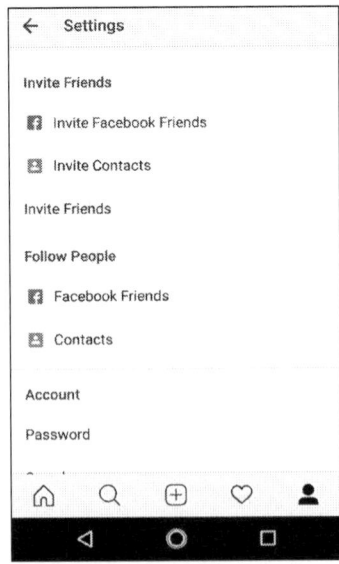

Figure 7.8: Configuring Settings

You can invite friends to join Instagram from your Facebook circle or your Contacts. You can change your account password.

Scroll down the Settings page to see more options that you can configure.

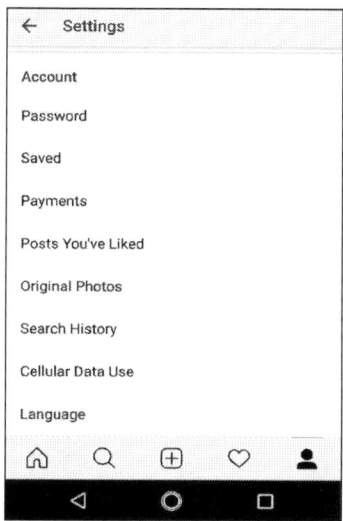

Figure 7.9: *More Settings Options*

You can turn on the **Private Account** button if you want to make your account private. Alternatively, you can choose the **Account Privacy** option and then turn your account into a private one.

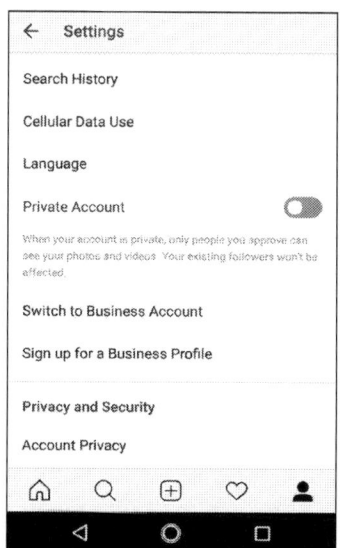

Figure 7.10: *Account Privacy Options*

You can learn more about private accounts and how it affects your posts, at this link:

https://help.instagram.com/243810329323104/?helpref=hc_ fnav&bc[0]=Instagram%20Help&bc[1]=Using%20 Instagram&bc[2]=Your%20Profile

Like other mobile apps, the Instagram app on your phone will show push notifications. You can choose what kind of notifications (if any) you want to allow.

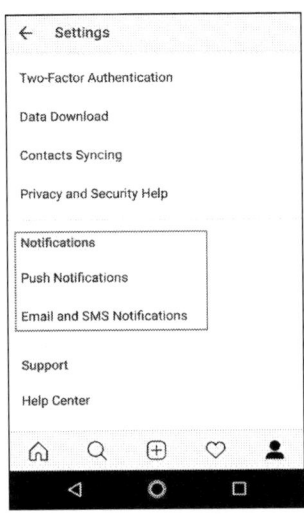

Figure 7.11: Configuring Notifications

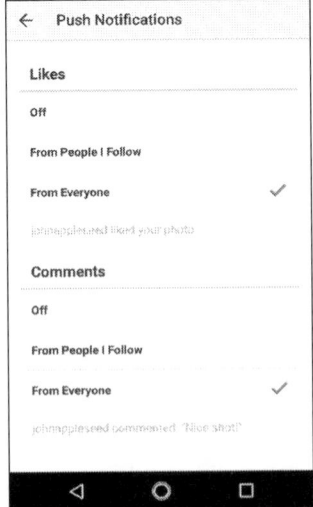

Figure 7.12: Push Notifications

Instagram Stories

On August 2, 2016, Instagram introduced Stories, a feature that allowed users post photos and videos that lasted only 24 hours. By October 2016, over a 100 million Instagram users were creating and sharing stories. This number has now increased to 400 million in 2018.

Instagram Stories are seen in a bar at the top of your feed. Whenever a new story is available for viewing in an account, it will show a colorful ring around the profile photo. Tapping on the profile photo will bring up the story in full- screen, showing all the content, the person has posted in the last 24 hours. The content will appear in chronological order from oldest to newest. Unlike regular posts, there are no likes or public comments on stories. You can send a message to the story creator for the story. The message will be seen only by the creator.

How-to - Create an Instagram Story

1. To create a story on Instagram, tap a new "+" icon at the top left-hand corner of the screen. Alternatively, reveal the story camera by swiping left.

2. Tap the circle button at the bottom of the screen to take photos or tap and hold to record a video.

3. You can also upload content created within the last 24 hours from your smartphone camera roll. To do this, simply swipe up on the stories camera, and you'll see the latest content from your camera roll, appear at the bottom of your screen. From here, simply select the content you'd like to add to your story.

4. Create the story content using photos and videos.

5. Edit the photos or videos with text or add a drawing. If you hit the pen icon, there are three types of pens. Add stickers to your story by tapping the Stickers button (a smiley face in the top right of the screen). You can add readymade hashtags to your story.

6. If you wish, you can add a location to the story.

7. Tap Save to save your Story. Tap **Send To**, to directly send it to one or more Instagram users.

8. Tap the **Your Story** button to share your Story.

Privacy settings of your account will be applied to your stories too. If you set your account to private, your story can be seen only by your followers.

However, if you want anyone to not see it, even if they follow you, it is possible to hide your entire story from them.

Instagram Stories are a great way for businesses and brands to reach out to users and grow their market.

For example, The New York Public Library is using Instagram Stories to bring classic novels to your smartphone:

https://www.theverge.com/2018/8/22/17768448/new-york-public-library-classic-novels-instagram-stories-alice-in-wonderland

Tip:

To use readymade templates for creating stories, check this link: **https://blog.bufferapp.com/instagram-stories-templates**

IGTV

When Instagram first introduced the video feature in 2013, the duration of clips was limited to 15 seconds in length. With time, Instagram realized the increasing attraction of video for users and increased the duration to 60 seconds.

In August 2014, Instagram launched Hyperlapse, a mobile app that enabled users to produce hyperlapse and time-lapse videos.

In June 2018, Instagram went even further, and launched an app for Android and iOS devices with longer form videos called IGTV. It offers a whole new video streaming experience on-the-go. Using this, some creators will be able to upload videos that are up to an hour in length. However, most creators will be capped at 10 minutes per video. The videos on IGTV will also appear in a vertical format, which is ideal for mobile devices.

Content starts playing immediately when you open the app. This includes videos of users that you follow in the main Instagram app. There will also be sections in the IGTV app called *For You, Following, Popular* and *Continue Watching*.

You can download the app from Google Play Store or Apple App Store. If you already have Instagram app signed-in on your phone, you get an option to sign into IGTV with the same account.

Tip:

https://adespresso.com/blog/instagram-tips-and-tricks-from-the-pros-in-2018/

Deleting Your Account

Deleting your account will cause your profile, photos, videos, comments, likes and followers to be permanently removed. If you need a short break from Twitter, you can temporarily disable your account and then resume. In this case, your profile, photos, comments and likes will be hidden until you reactivate it by logging back in.

Disabling or deleting an account has to be done via mobile browser or Web browser, and cannot be done through the app.

To temporarily disable your account:

1. Log into your Instagram account.

2. Tap or click profile icon in the top right and then select **Edit Profile**.

3. Scroll down, then tap or click **Temporarily disable my account** in the bottom right.

4. Select an option from the drop-down menu next to **Why are you disabling your account?**

5. Re-enter your password. The option to disable your account will be displayed only after you select a reason from the menu.

6. Tap or click **Temporarily Disable Account**.

To permanently delete your account:

1. Navigate to the **Delete Your Account** page.

2. Select an option from the drop-down menu next to **Why are you deleting your account?**

3. Re-enter your password. The option to permanently delete your account will be displayed only after you select a reason from the menu.

4. Click or tap **Permanently delete my account.**

Summary

*   Instagram is a social media platform primarily designed for photo-sharing.
*   Using Instagram, you can follow other people with similar interests, upload and share a picture from your phone, capture and share a live picture, create a live story and share it, like and/or share others' posts and more.
*   Instagram accounts can be public or private.
*   Instagram stories are used to create and share stories made up of photos, videos, stickers, and text and last only 24 hours.
*   Instagram now allows longer videos through a stand alone app called IGTV.

Chapter 7 Quiz

1. You can add a public comment or like on an Instagram post. [True/False]
2. You can add a public comment or like on an Instagram story. [True/False]
3. IGTV is a standalone app by Instagram that enables you to create or view longer videos. [True/False]
4. If a profile/account is set to private, only approved followers will be able to view or search your content. [True/False]

CHAPTER 8
Pinterest

I n this chapter, we take a look at Pinterest.

Objectives

By the end of this chapter, you will be able to:

- Understand the Pinterest platform
- Identify key features of Pinterest
- Sign Up for a Pinterest account
- Create your Pinboard
- Follow other users
- Showcase your tried pins
- Learn about Pinterest for mobile
- Understand Pinterest for business

Introduction to Pinterest

Pinterest is a visual social network platform comprising Web and mobile application, designed to discover information on the World Wide Web.

It acts like an online pinboard, enabling people to collect and share images, GIFs, and videos in the form of *pins*. Users can create as many boards for their pins as they want. For example, if you like collecting pictures of cute puppies, you can create a board and label it *Puppies*. Alongside this board, you can create other boards such as *Cinema Stills*, Books, Popular Quotes and so on, based on your interests.

Evolution and Growth

Founded in March 2010, Pinterest has been the fastest independently launched site to reach 10 million unique monthly visitors.

As of June 2018, this platform has 200 million monthly active visitors across the globe. Over 50% of these users are from outside the USA. Pinterest is more popular among women, with 70% of the total users being women. Refer to *Figure 8.1* to see some sample boards.

Figure 8.1: *Sample Boards on Pinterest*

Users on this platform interact with each other by liking, commenting, and *repining* each other's stuff.

What can users pin on Pinterest? There are a lot of things that users can pin on Pinterest. Businesses, for example, can focus on visual content including not just photos but also articles, infographics, and even more.

Features of Pinterest

Using Pinterest, you can

- Save ideas, inspirations, or just something you like in the form of pins.
- Save each pin to a board and organize your boards.
- Add, edit, or delete pins.
- Move, copy or delete pins in bulk.
- Repin others' pins.
- Follow other people or boards.
- Use Promoted Pin options to help you reach your business goals.
- Showcase ideas, recipes, or projects that you have tried through *Tries*.
- Share your pins across other social media platforms or over email.
  And more

Now, let's use some of these features hands-on.

How-to: Create a Pinterest account and Profile

Pinterest is free to use, but like any other social network, you need an account to start using it.

1. Create a free account at Pinterest.com with an email and password or choose to create one from your existing Facebook or Google account.

Refer to Figure 8.2.

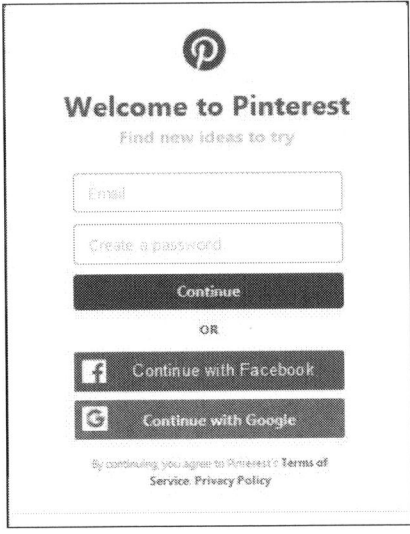

Figure 8.2: Creating an Account

2. Fill out the details such as your name, gender, language and country that you are prompted for. You will then be shown a screen with different categories of photos. Refer to *Figure 8.3*.

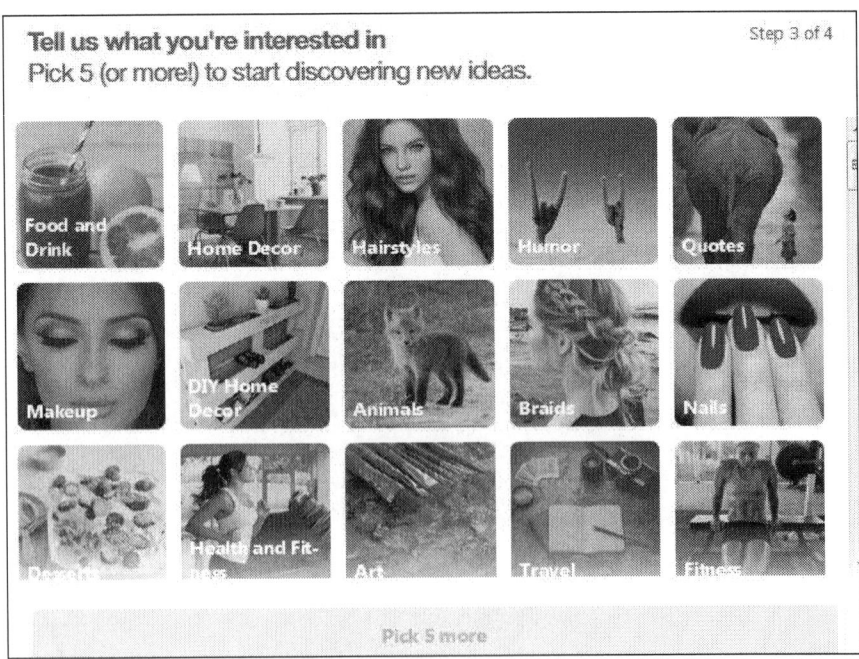

Figure 8.3: Choosing Interests

3. Pick at least five categories to follow so that Pinterest can start showing you personalized pins based on your interests. Once this is done, your account will be ready to go! You will see your name, profile picture, and a couple of icons in the top right corner. Towards the end, you will see three dots.

4. Click those dots, and then click **Edit Settings** to open your profile.

Figure 8.4 shows this option.

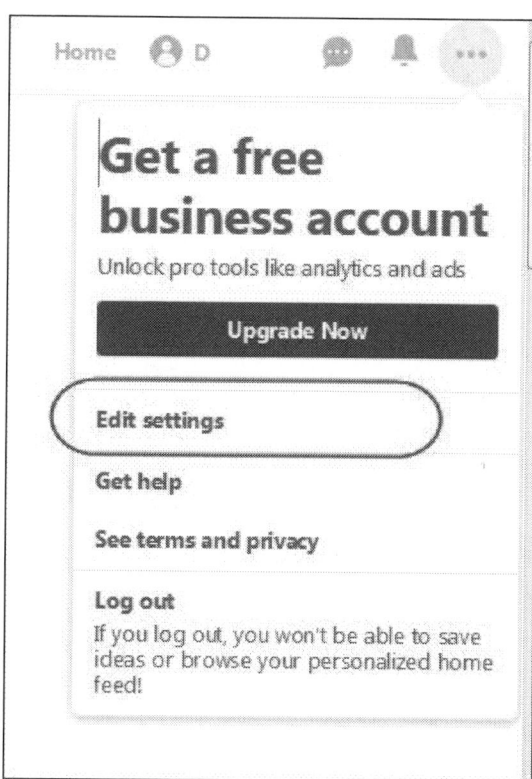

Figure 8.4: *Edit Settings Option*

You will be shown a page like *Figure 8.5*. Edit the information as desired.

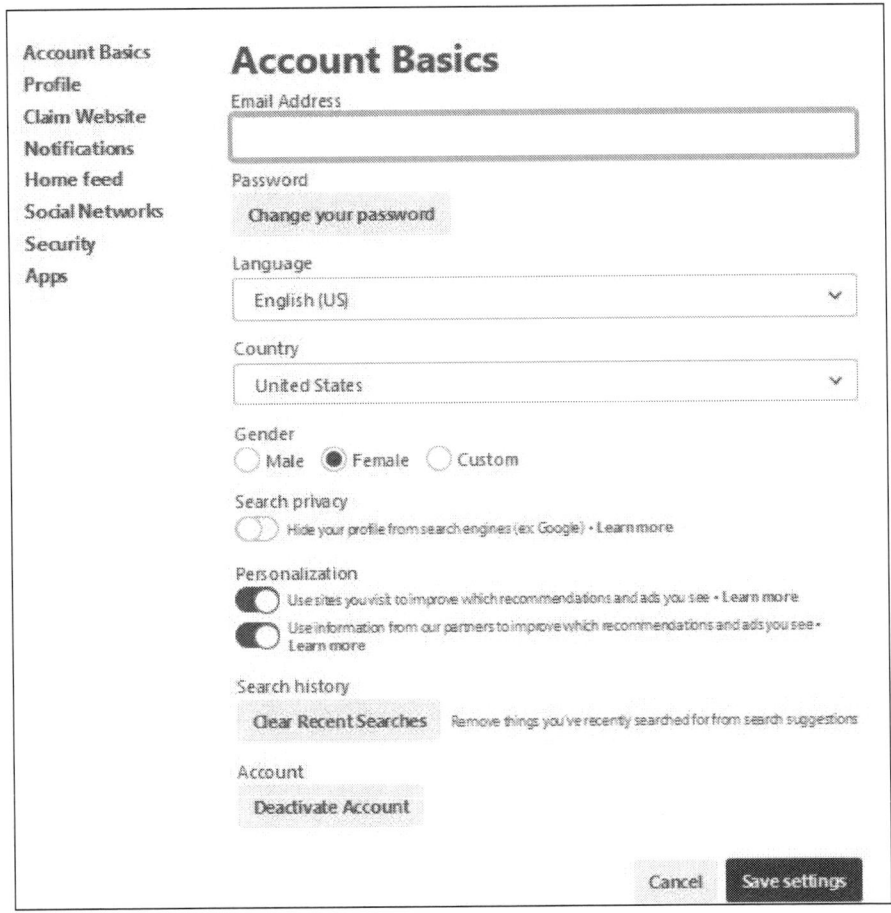

Figure 8.5: Editing Account Information

Once your profile is set, you can start pinning and creating boards.

How-to: Create Pins and Boards

1. To begin pinning from the Web, click either Home or Explore.

2. You will be shown popular pins in the categories you have
    chosen. Click on any picture. See *Figure 8.6*.

Figure 8.6: Exploring Pins

3. Each picture usually shows a caption and a source. The **Save**
    button on the top right allows you to pin the picture to your
    board. Since you don't have any board presently, you will be
    asked to create one. See *Figure 8.7*.

Figure 8.7: Creating Boards

4. As you can see, Pinterest has also suggested some names for your board. You can either choose one of them or type in your own.

5. Once you click **Save**, the picture will be saved as a Pin and will be part of the board you created.

Now, you can see four tabs:

Boards: Will display all the boards you create.

Pins: Will display all the items you pinned.

Tries: Will display all the pins that you tried for yourself and left feedback on. These may include, fitness tips, travel ideas, DIY ideas, recipes, and more.

Topics: Will display all the categories you have chosen.

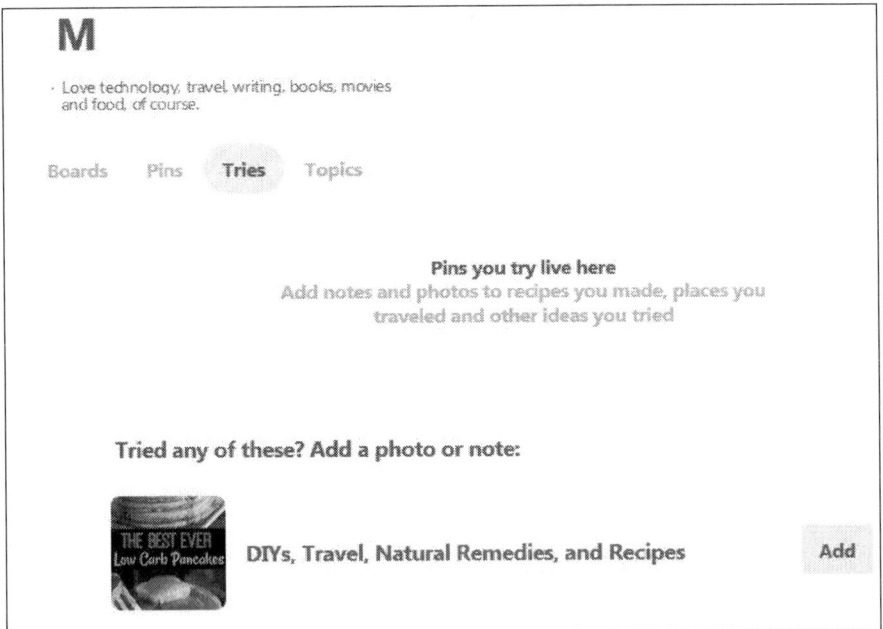

Figure 8.8: Tabs

6. You can also save pins from your computer. On your profile, click either **Pins** tab or **Boards** tab. Look for the **Create Pin** button or **Create Board** button to the far left of your

pins/boards. Select the image from your computer to upload it to the Web and then click **Upload Pin**.

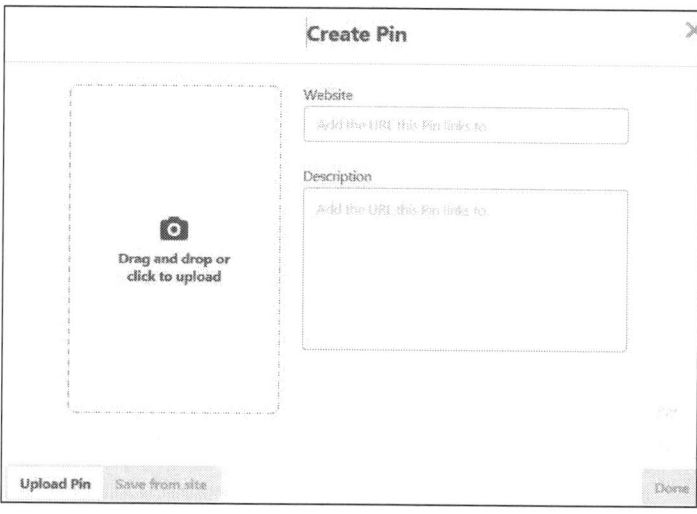

Figure 8.9: Creating a Pin

Once you have a few pins and boards ready, you can follow other Pinterest users.

How-to: Follow Other Users and Boards

1. Click any user profile (at the bottom of each picture posted by others, you will see the username who pinned it) and then click **Follow**. You can also find more people to follow by viewing the Followers of a specific Pinterest user.

   Refer *Figure 8.10*.

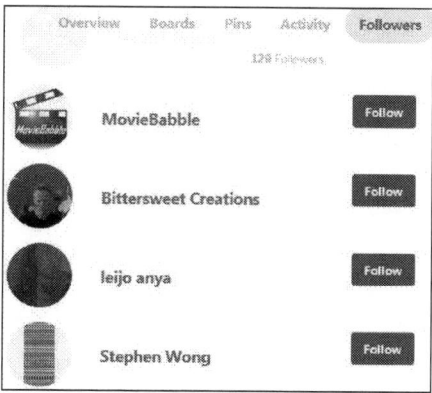

Figure 8.10: Following Other Pinterest Users

2. Suppose through a pin someone else had pinned to their board, you land upon that board and then you want to continue seeing more pins that get pinned to the board, you can just follow the board. Click **Follow** at the top corner of the board to follow it. Refer *Figure 8.11.*

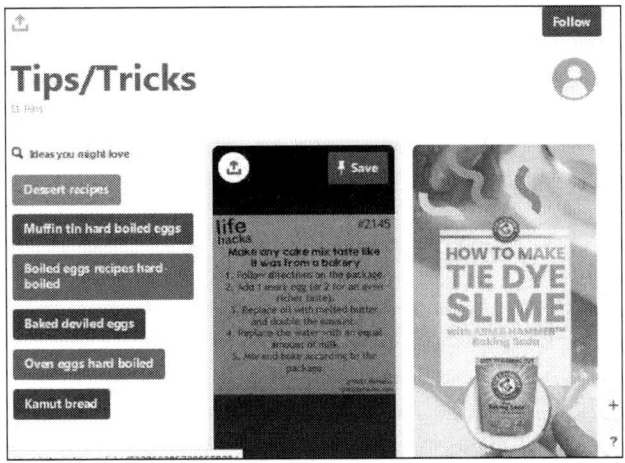

Figure 8.11: *Follow Button*

3. You can also share your pins and boards across other social media platforms or over email. Click a pin you saved earlier to a board. Click the arrow icon at the top left corner on the pin. You will be presented with options to share the pin across a variety of social media networks. Alternatively, if you want to send it to someone via email, you can just type out the email address. Refer *Figure 8.12.*

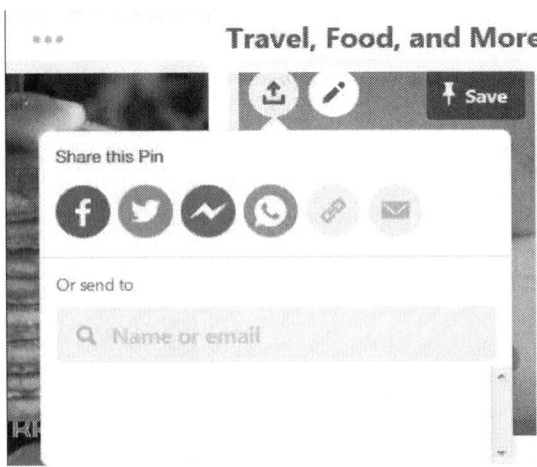

Figure 8.12: *Sharing Via Email*

4. Besides sharing individual pins, you can also share an entire board. Just like the pin, there's the share button ↥ atop the board which you can use to share the board with your social media circle or over e-mail.

How-to: Send and Receive Messages

Observe the top right corner of your account page. You will see several icons. The **Home** icon leads you to your homepage on Pinterest. The **Following** icon will show you the pins, people, boards, topics that you are following. **Explore** icon lets you explore Pinterest and search for interesting pins. The callout with the three dots represents the **Messaging** feature using which you can send and receive messages. Refer *Figure 8.13*.

Figure 8.13: Messaging via Pinterest

1. Click the **Messaging** icon. You will see two buttons. Refer *Figure 8.14*.

Figure 8.14: Messages and Compose Buttons

2. Click **Compose** to select the recipient to whom the message is to be sent and then start writing a message. You can select the name of other Pinterest users who are following you or your boards or invite someone who is not yet on Pinterest. You can add up to a maximum of nine users in the To: section. Once the recipient is specified, you can start typing your message.

3. Alternatively, if you are following a user, just click their profile and then click the **Message** button to send a message.

4. When others send you messages, you will be able to view them. The **Callout** icon will indicate that you have messages waiting to be viewed. If you aren't following the person who has sent you a message, you will not be able to view the message unless you approve the message request by clicking **Accept**. Refer *Figure 8.15*.

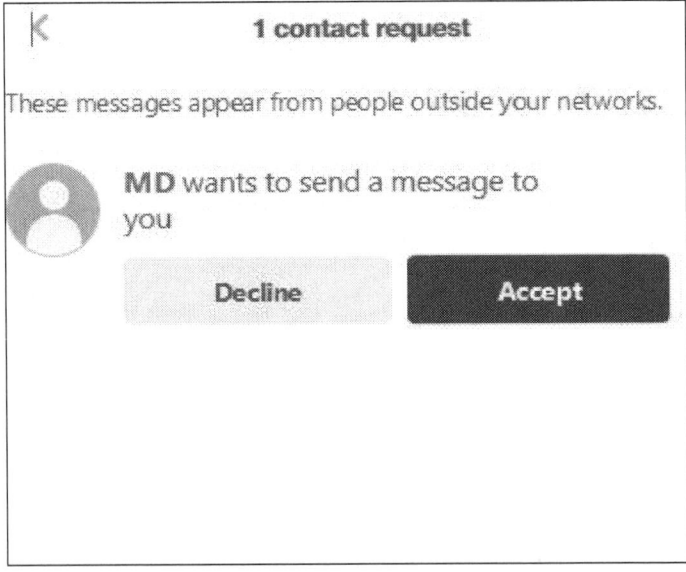

Figure 8.15: Accepting Contact Requests

How-to: Configure Notifications

1. Click the bell icon. It represents **Notifications** regarding pins, boards, new follows, and more, that Pinterest sends you. You can customize how you want to receive your notifications, if at all you do want to receive. You can, if you wish, turn off all notifications, though this is not recommended.

Refer *Figure 8.16* to view the various options.

Account basics	**Notifications**	
Profile		
Claim website	We'll always let you know about important changes, but you pick what else you want to hear about. **Learn more**	
Notifications		
Home feed	On Pinterest	Edit
Social networks	Activity from other people on Pinterest	
Security		
Apps	By email	Edit
	Everything (except emails you've turned off)	
	By push notification	Edit
	Everything (except push notifications you've turned off)	

Figure 8.16: Notifications

If you use the Pinterest mobile app, you can configure how you wish to receive Push notifications on your mobile.

How-to: Move, Edit, or Delete Pins and Boards

1. It is possible to move, edit, or delete pins and boards. Click the specific pin you want to edit. You will see an Edit button at the top left corner. Refer *Figure 8.17*.

Figure 8.17: Edit Button

2. Click the **Edit** button. You will be shown various options to edit it. For example, you can move the pin to another board by clicking the board drop-down and selecting another board. You can specify a section under the **Section** drop-down. You can edit the existing **Description** and write something different. You can also delete the pin by clicking the **Delete** button at the bottom.

Figure 8.18: Editing Pins

3. Exercise caution when using this because once you delete a pin, you won't be able to recover it. This is the reason Pinterest also confirms whether you really want to delete the pin. Refer *Figure 8.19.*

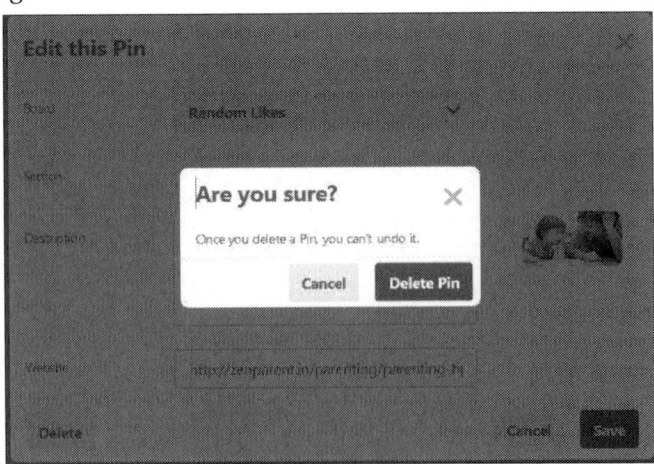

Figure 8.19: Confirmation of Pin Deletion

Rich Pins

A Rich Pin is a feature of Pinterest that can be useful for Websites and businesses. It provides more context about an idea because it shows extra information directly on a Pin. Rich Pins can add additional details to Pins from your website.

To configure rich pins for your website, you will need to add metadata to your site and apply for rich pins. You can read more about the process at this link: **https://developers.pinterest.com/docs/ rich-pins/overview/**

There are four types of Rich Pins: product, article, app install, and recipe.

- **Product Pins** are used to facilitate easy shopping by including real-time pricing, availability, and where to buy your product.
- **Recipe Pins** display ingredients, cooking times, and serving sizes.
- **Article Pins** help Pinners save stories that matter to them. Each Article Pin shows a headline, author, and story description.
- **App Install Pins** These Pins show an install button so people can download your app without leaving Pinterest. For now, App Pins are only compatible with iOS.

Pinterest Mobile App

Pinterest mobile app is available for iOS devices as well as Android devices at the App Store (iTunes) and Google Play Store (for Android phones) respectively.

The Pinterest app is a slimmed down version of the site version. Certain features are different on the mobile app. For instance, previews of Descriptions are shorter on smartphones.

Pinterest for Business

Pinterest is nowadays not just a visual social network tool, but also a search engine curated by users of Pinterest and Pinterest's search algorithm. In other words, Pinterest is a social site crossed with a search engine. It can greatly help visual search and discovery.

As a business, you can leverage this to your advantage to attract potential customers. There are many search engine optimizations that you can create in Pinterest. You can learn to optimize Pinterest search results for the search terms that customers type. This can improve your business search rankings on Pinterest, Google, and Bing too.

Pinterest pin search results are influenced by the keywords you add to your pin's description, the number of repins that a pin has, and whether it's a rich pin. It also helps if the pin comes from a URL with the keyword mentioned in it.

Promoted Pin is a special feature for businesses. Promoted pins are regular Pins that are paid for to reach potential customers. Using this feature, your desired audience can see your pins in relevant search results and feeds. Currently, this feature is not available for India.

You can use hashtags to promote your products in promoted pins. Pinterest allows at most one hashtag in your pin description for the promoted pin to be approved. Hashtags are the only clickable on the desktop and mobile internet versions of Pinterest. They will not work on mobile apps.

Tips:

Check out these links to make the most from Pinterest for Business.

How to Use Pinterest for Business: 8 Strategies You Need to Know How to Use Pinterest for Business

Pinterest for Business:20 Strategies for Pinterest Marketing in 2018 How to Search Optimize your Pins on Pinterest

Summary

- Pinterest is a visual social network platform comprising web and mobile application, designed to discover information on the World Wide Web.

- Pinterest enables users to collect and share images, GIFs, and videos in the form of *pins* and *boards*.

- Users can organize boards, edit, move, copy, and delete pins.

- Users can share their pins across other social media platforms or even email.

- Messages feature allows you to message other Pinterest users who follow at least one of your boards.
- Pinterest mobile app is available for iOS as well as Android devices.
- Pinterest offers many features for businesses.

Chapter 8 Quiz

1. As a Pinterest user, you can use Pinterest Messages feature to contact _____.

   A) people you follow.

   B) only people who you follow and follow you back.

   C) people who follow at least one of your boards.

   D) anybody who is using Pinterest.

2. Identify which of the following is not a factor, when it comes to Pinterest pin search results?

   A) The keywords you put into your pin's description.

   B) The number of repins that the pin has.

   C) Whether it's a rich pin.

   D) The vertical size of the pin.

3. Which of the following factors influence board search results? (Choose all that apply.)

   A) How frequently you pin to that board.

   B) How many followers you have.

   C) Keywords in the name of your board.

   D) Keywords used in your board's description.

4. There are three types of Rich Pins.   [True/False]

5. Once you delete a pin, you cannot recover it. [True/False]

CHAPTER 9
LinkedIn

In this chapter, we take a look at LinkedIn.

Objectives

By the end of this chapter, you will be able to:

- Understand the Linked platform
- Identify key features of LinkedIn
- Sign Up for a LinkedIn account
- Create a LinkedIn Profile
- Connect with people on LinkedIn
- Use the LinkedIn mobile app
- Delete or close your account

Introduction to LinkedIn

LinkedIn is a social networking platform for business and employment. Founded in December 2002 and formally launched in May 2003, the platform has now garnered LinkedIn reached 500 million users, across 200 countries. After US, India, Brazil, Great Britain and Canada have the highest number of LinkedIn users.

LinkedIn was acquired by Microsoft in 2016.

Through LinkedIn, working professionals, aspiring job seekers, and employers can connect with one another. Upon signing up at LinkedIn, a user creates a profile, which is structured like a curriculum vitae or resumé.

Users can elaborate on their work experience, education, and training, skills, and optionally, a personal photo. They may also list their interests, that could help them further in their career. For example, a database developer may also be keenly interested in **artificial intelligence (AI)** and may want to pursue an alternate career in AI. He/she can then list AI as their interests.

When a user connects to a person through LinkedIn, it is called as *making a connection*. Users can invite anyone (whether a site member or not) to become a connection. However, LinkedIn prefers that you connect with people you know from your school/college, business area or workplace or you know the person as a friend.

Account Restriction or Suspension

While sending out invites, among the other options, there's one that says "I don't know <person name". If you click this option, it can possibly annoy the person who receives the invitation from a stranger. So, use this option wisely and judiciously.

If the person to whom you sent an invite, also called an invitee, selects **I don't know** or **Spam** on receiving your invitation to connect, this can count against you. If many such incidents occur, your account can get restricted or even closed.

LinkedIn Statistics (2018):

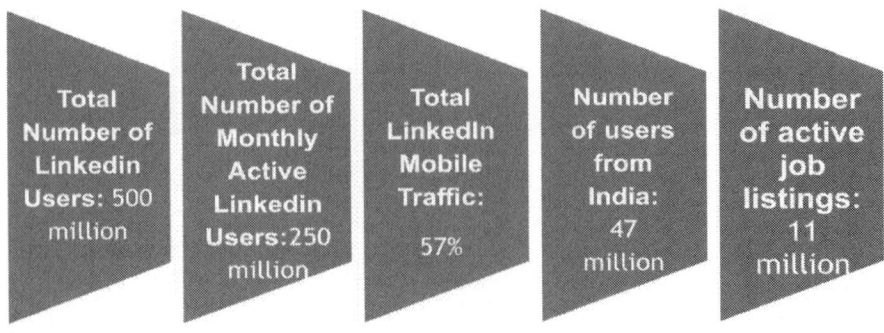

LinkedIn Terminology

Term	Definition
Connections	People whom you invite, or people who have invited you.
Second-Degree Connections	Connections of connections.
Third-Degree Connections	Connections of second-degree connections.
Network	Group of users whom you can reach out to your connections and those users who are more than three degrees away from you but are willing to be contacted without referral. It also includes members of groups you share.
Profile	Represents your public persona on LinkedIn. This is what other users see when they find you through a search.
Endorsements	A one-click feature where your connections can recognize or acknowledge your skills and expertise.
Recommendation	Like an endorsement, it is written by one connection regarding another, recommending his/her work and includes remarks about exemplary work done. Recommendations are visible to all users who can see the endorsee's profile.
InMails	Internal LinkedIn emails. You need a premium (paid) service to send such emails, unless the recipient has configured their settings to allow anyone to send them mails.
Trending Topics	Popular topics for the day. This appears on the left pane and is collated using built-in algorithms.
Smart Replies	Automated suggested responses below an open conversation in LinkedIn Messaging based on the messages that were most recently sent.

Native Videos	You can upload native videos directly to LinkedIn through the LinkedIn mobile app.

Table 9.1

What can you do on LinkedIn?

- Create a professional profile.
- Connect with people.
    - o Obtain introductions to the connections of connections (termed *second-degree connections*) and connections of second-degree connections (termed *third-degree connections*)
    - o Search for second-degree connections who work at a specific company they are interested in, and then ask a specific first-degree connection in common for an introduction
- Look for jobs, people and business opportunities recommended by someone in one's contact network.
- List job openings in case you are an employer and look for potential candidates.
- Share video with text and filters with the introduction of LinkedIn Video.
- Follow different organizations.
- Save or bookmark jobs you might be interested in.
- *Like* and *congratulate* other's updates and new jobs or job milestones (such as anniversaries) or wish them on their birthday or other important occasions.
- Write posts, blogs, and articles within the LinkedIn platform to share with their network.
- Research graduate schools and their background, before you apply there.
- Create/join groups based on your alma mater, previous workplaces, or interests.

Benefits of being on LinkedIn

LinkedIn offers both aspiring job seekers and employers a vast number of benefits. Some of these are as follows:

- You can discover great job openings.

- You can connect with hiring managers. If you are a hiring manager, it helps you connect with prospective candidates.

- You can learn more about candidates who have applied to job openings that you have posted as an employer. A latest career research revealed that number of employers using social media to screen prospective employees is at an all-time high. 93% of hiring managers search LinkedIn for recruits, according to a survey by career website Jobvite.

- You can discover other companies and gain awareness about the industry.

- You can easily locate other professionals in the same industry.

- Write posts and share through LinkedIn's publishing platform.

- Gain from the knowledge of your network.

- Easily search for jobs and learn about exciting career opportunities.

Creating a Profile

According to LinkedIn,

"Your LinkedIn profile is a professional landing page for you to manage your own, personal brand. It's a great way for you to tell people who you are and what you do by displaying a general history of your professional experiences and achievements. Use your LinkedIn profile to add a personal touch that a typical resume or CV may not reflect."

How-to: Create a Profile

1. First, open the LinkedIn website. You will see a page similar to *Figure 9.1*.

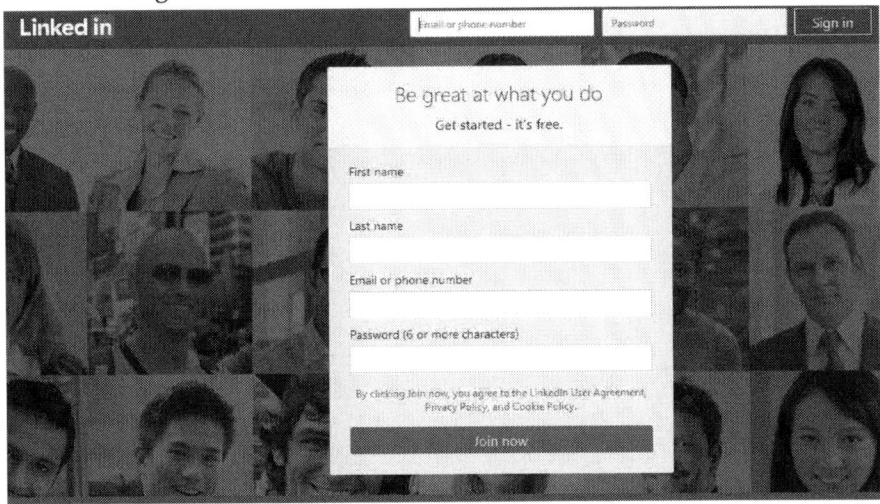

Figure 9.1: LinkedIn Home Page

2. Type your First and last name, email address or phone number, and a password you wish to use. Remember the password well, you'll need it frequently later.

3. Click **Join now**.

4. Enter additional information that you are prompted for, such as your country and postal code.

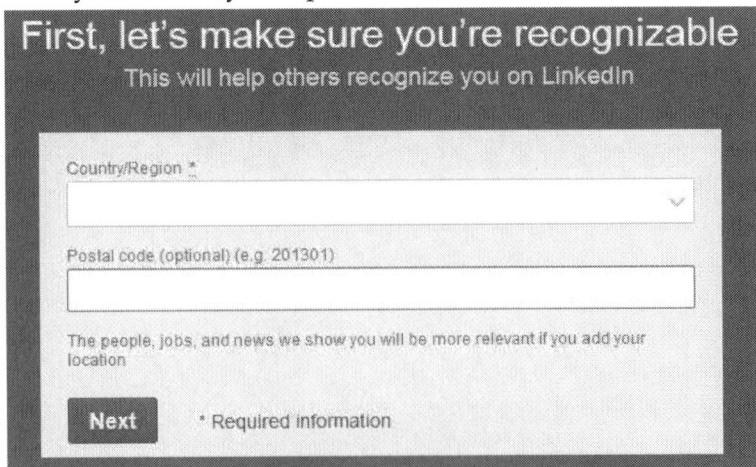

Figure 9.2: Adding Account Information

5. Complete the registration procedure by following all the steps.

6. Next, add and fill in the following sections in your profile from the drop- down on the top part of your profile, also called as an introduction card:

   - Background
   - Skills
   - Accomplishments

To do this:

   i. Click the **Me** icon at the top of your homepage and then, click **View profile**.

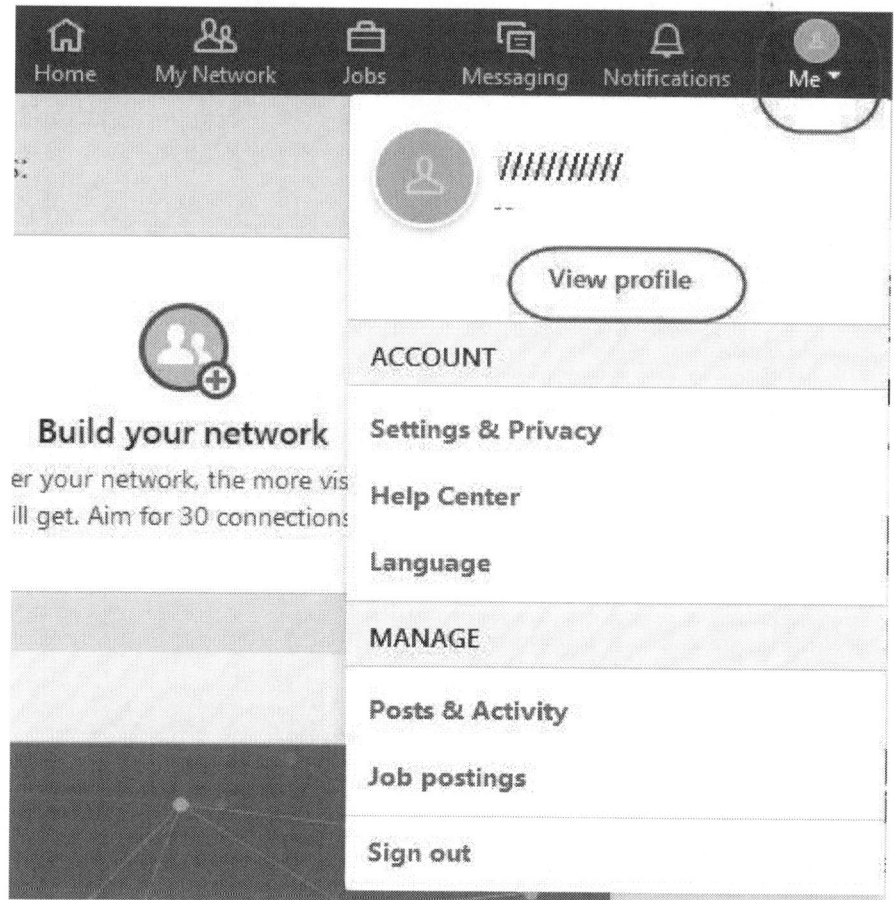

Figure 9.3: View Profile Button

ii. Click *Add profile* section in your introduction card. Start by filling out various fields one by one.

Education

Add your school and/or college qualifications here. It is up to you, exactly how much information you want to include.

(Work) Experience

A brief summary of your work experience. If you have worked in more than one company, include the details and the roles and responsibilities that you handled at each. Make sure to keep it short and succinct.

Featured Skills

Important skills that you possess must be highlighted here. These can include both functional and behavioral skills. For example, Public Relations, Project Management, Creative Writing, Training Delivery, Enterprise Software, Software Testing, and so on.

i. Add a profile photo.

ii. Add a Website. You can include up to three links in your profile.

iii. Add your Phone number, social media accounts, and birthday if you wish. Note that you can control the visibility of these details.

Tips:

Check out these sites on how to create a winning profile.

https://www.themuse.com/advice/the-31-best-linkedin-profile-tips-for-job-seekers

http://time.com/money/5077954/linkedin-profile-tips-resume/

Once your profile is ready, you can start adding connections.

Adding Connections

You build connections on LinkedIn by means of *Invitations*. When you send an invite to another person and they accept your invitation, they become your first-degree connections.

If the person to whom you send an invitation is not on LinkedIn member, they will be prompted to join LinkedIn so that they can accept your invitation.

Refer the earlier *Table 9.1* to know what are the different degrees of connections.

You can import your mobile address book into the LinkedIn app to identify your contacts who are already using LinkedIn.

Sync your mobile address book with LinkedIn to continually discover new connections, as and when you add new contacts.

You can also withdraw an invitation that you've sent, which will stop the recipient from receiving any further reminder emails to accept the invitation. The person you invited will not get any notification that you have canceled the invitation.

The total number of connections a member is allowed to have is 30,000.

How-to: Add Connections

You can add connections using any one of the following ways:

- Click the **Connect** button on a member's profile page.

Figure 9.4: Adding Connections

- Click on **Connect** button, to the right of the member's information on the search results page.

Showing 1,045,434 results

Bill Stayart · 2nd
Humble Communicator-Dependable Forcastable Sales/Mgnt./Dir.A Winner-Mutually Profi...
Greater Los Angeles Area
Past: Sr. Sales Engineer at Simplex Time Recorder

Connect

Will Humphreys · 2nd 🔲
Healthcare & Digital Marketing Technology
Panama City, Florida Area

Connect

William Harrison · 2nd
IT Service Management Consulting at WRH zSERVICES, LLC
Houston, Texas Area

Connect

Figure 9.5: Adding Connections via Search Results Page

- Click the **Connect** button below the member's name on the *People You May Know page*. Refer to *Figure 9.6*.

People you may know

Josh Anderson
Demand Generation – SEO – PPC – Marketing Technology

Connect

Darren Hunt BSc(Hons),
Managing Director at Two Fold United Electrical & Mechanical

Connect

Figure 9.6: People You May Know

- Search your email address book, to find contacts or invite them using their email address.

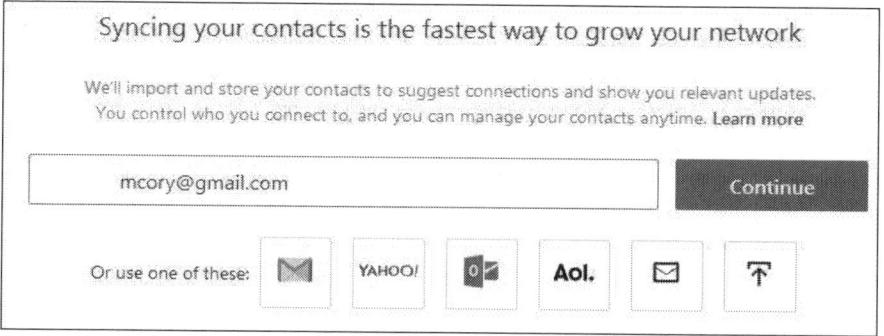

Figure 9.7: Inviting Contacts via Email

- Tap the **Connect** button on a member's profile in the LinkedIn mobile website or app, whom you want to connect with.

Messaging Your Connections

You can send private messages or mails (also called InMail) to your connections.

How-to: Send Messages through the Chat Window

1. Click the **Messaging** icon at the top of your LinkedIn homepage.

Figure 9.8: Messaging

2. Click the **Compose a new message** icon on the left rail.

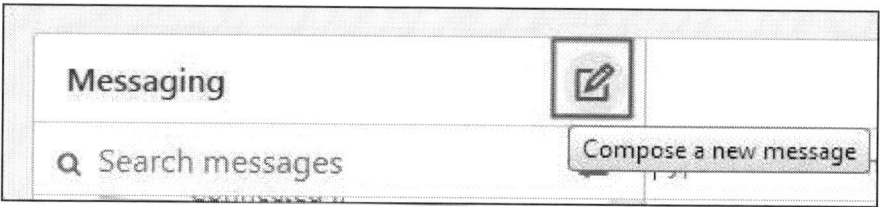

Figure 9.9: Composing Messages

3. Type the name(s) of the person(s) whom you wish to send the message in the Type a name field. You can add up to 50 people to the conversation.

Figure 9.10: Typing Names of Persons

4. Write your message in the text box. You can add images, GIFs, or attach files along with the message.

5. Click **Send** to send the message or press the **Enter** key to send the message.

   o If Click to Send is enabled (which is the default), pressing the *Enter* key allows you to add a new paragraph in your message.

   o If **Press Enter to Send** is enabled, pressing *Shift + Enter* allows you to add a new paragraph within your message.

Alternatively, you can send a message from your connections page by locating the connection whom you want to message from your connections list and then clicking **Message** next to their name.

Similarly, you can also send emails via LinkedIn to your connections through the InMail option.

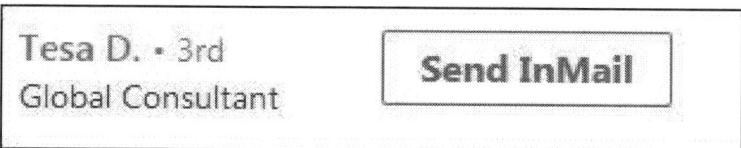

Figure 9.11: InMail

Make Optimum Use of LinkedIn

https://www.linkedinsights.com/18-enormously-useful-linkedin-hacks-2017/https://blog.hubspot.com/sales/hidden-linkedin-hacks-revealed-slidesharehttps://www.forbes.com/sites/williamarruda/2014/03/04/22-linkedin-secrets-linkedin-wont-tell-you/#4db187bc27fehttps://www.yesware.com/blog/linkedin-profile/

Using the LinkedIn Mobile App

The LinkedIn mobile app is available at the Apple store as well as Google Play. This app is a mobile based version of LinkedIn.

The mobile app facilitates easy profile editing while being on the move, viewing and engaging with connections' updates, and or even changing your account settings. You can also easily create and share updates.

Moreover, you can use the Messaging feature in the LinkedIn app, which is easier to use on your phone, as compared to the desktop equivalent.

Based on your phone OS, go to the respective store, download the app, and start using it.

Closing or deleting your LinkedIn account

When you close or delete your account, your profile and all the related LinkedIn information will no longer exist.

How-to: Close Your Account

There are two ways to close your LinkedIn account.

1) The first approach is by using the **Settings & Privacy** page:

    i. Sign in to LinkedIn.

    ii. Click the **Me** icon on the top.

Figure 9.12: Settings & Privacy Option

    iii. Select **Settings & Privacy** from the drop-down.

    iv. Go to the **Account management** section of the **Account** tab.

    v. Click **Change** next to **Closing your LinkedIn account**.

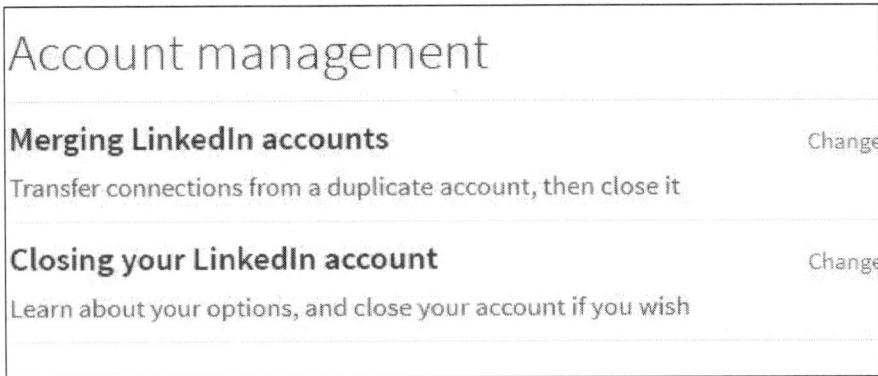

Figure 9.13: Closing Your Account

vi. Select the reason why you wish to close your account and then, click **Next**.

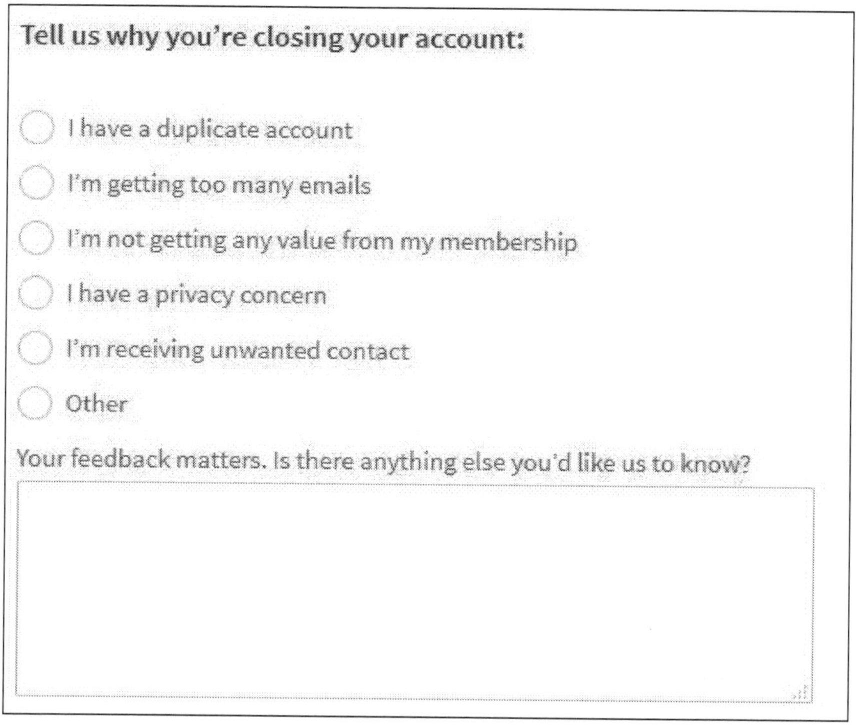

Tell us why you're closing your account:

◯ I have a duplicate account

◯ I'm getting too many emails

◯ I'm not getting any value from my membership

◯ I have a privacy concern

◯ I'm receiving unwanted contact

◯ Other

Your feedback matters. Is there anything else you'd like us to know?

Figure 9.14: Specify Reason for Closing

vii. In the next screen, type in your account password and click **Close account**.

2) The second approach is by using the **Close Account** page **https://www.linkedin.com/psettings/account-management/ close-action-needed.**

Once you close your account:

- Your profile will not be visible on LinkedIn.

- You will no longer have access to your connections, or any information that are part of your account.

- You'll lose all recommendations and endorsements you've collected on your LinkedIn profile.

- Search engines such as Google, Bing, and others may display your information temporarily because of the way in which they collect and update their search data.

You may want to download a copy of your data before you close your account with us.

> **Note:** In case you own premium membership, are owner of a LinkedIn group, or have a premium account license, you must resolve those accounts first, in order to close your Basic account.

What if you change your mind about deleting your account?

If you have second thoughts about closing your account and want to continue using your account, you can reopen it provided the time lapsed is less than 20 days. However, although you may be successful in reopening your account, you will not be to retain the following information:

- Group memberships
- Endorsements
- Recommendations
- Pending invitations
- Companies and influencers whom you have been following

These details are permanently lost, once you submit a request to close your account. So, even if less than 20 days have passed since you submitted the close request, you will lose all this information.

Summary

- LinkedIn is a social networking platform for business and employment that helps working professionals, aspiring job seekers, and employers to connect with one another.

- Users create a profile on LinkedIn, elaborating their work experience, education and training, skills, and optionally, a personal photo.

- When a user connects to a person through LinkedIn, it is called as making a connection. Users can send invitations to other people (LinkedIn users or even people who are not on LinkedIn) to become a connection.

- LinkedIn offers a vast number of benefits to both job seekers and employers.

- Users can create connections using a variety of ways, the easiest of which is by using the **Connect** button on a member's profile.

- Users can send private messages and occasionally even emails through LinkedIn.

Chapter 9 Quiz

1. You can create only 100 connections in LinkedIn. [True/False]

2. You can add your personal information such as your marital status, wedding anniversary, reminders in your LinkedIn profile. [True/False]

3. To send private messages to one or more people, you click the _____ icon at the top of your LinkedIn profile.

4. You can sync your mobile address book with LinkedIn. [True/False]

5. You can upload native videos directly to LinkedIn through the LinkedIn mobile app. [True/False]

CHAPTER 10
Social Media Management Tools

In this chapter, we take a look at the different social media management tools.

Objectives

By the end of this chapter, you will be able to:

- Identify various social media management tools
- Learn about the features offered by various social media management tools

Social Media Management Tools

Considering that there are a plethora of social media platforms and sites today such as Facebook, Twitter, Instagram, and so on, it can become difficult to manage them on a day-to-day basis. This is even more so if you have different social accounts for personal and professional purposes.

Hence, to make it easier for you to work with your various social media accounts in an efficient and organized manner, there are social media management tools available today. These tools also provide several other advantages such as:

- Quicker and efficient response to feedback (complaints and criticism).
- Gathering vital information from your social media followers and customer base for later analysis.
- Gathering data on customer behavior and satisfaction.
- Streamlining team collaboration to avoid redundancy in responses.

Let's now look at some of the most popular social media management tools.

- HootSuite
- MAVSocial
- ZohoSocial
- IFTTT
- SocialPilot
- TweetDeck
- Buffer
- AgoraPulse
- SproutSocial

Hootsuite is a social media management tool that helps businesses plan and implement outstanding social media strategies.

Using Hootsuite, they can collaboratively schedule posts across their social media accounts such as LinkedIn, Facebook, Twitter, Instagram, and so on. This tool also helps in content curation and social media analytics.

It enables your company to monitor social conversations, in order to determine what the public is talking about your brand, competitors, and so on.

It offers a social media dashboard to track and manage the different social media profiles of your business.

Consider that as a globally growing business, you now have four Instagram accounts, two Twitter accounts, and six Facebook Pages.

It would be cumbersome and tricky for your team to manage them efficiently. This is where HootSuite can help.

This tool helps you manage multiple accounts through one single dashboard.

Who is Using HootSuite?

Its customers include the University of Cambridge, Visa, Nokia, Accor Hotels, Wiley, and many more companies. It is used by over 16 million users, in over 175 countries across the world.

Hootsuite Pricing Plans

Hootsuite is available in four pricing models. You can sign up for a 30-day free trial for the first two plans and request a demo for the other two.

- Professional
- Team
- Business
- Enterprise

MAVSOCIAL ⟩✖⟨

MavSocial is another popular social media management tool. Its features include content curation, scheduling and automation of social media posts, managing social media interactions and conversations, and facilitating collaboration.

Visual content forms a crucial part of any social media marketing strategy. MavSocial helps makes it easier for you to publish visual content. It offers a centralized platform capable of storing tons of photos, videos, infographics, and more, and can be accessed anytime. This tool also makes available for you access to over 70 million royalty-free images from stock sites such as Getty Images, Bigstock, Pixabay, Giphy, and so on. This helps you save time and effort.

Who is Using MavSocial?

It is used by a number of large corporations based across the world, such as GrowMap, Market Core Media, and more.

MavSocial Pricing Plans

MavSocial offers two plans: Small Business Edition (Free) and Enterprise and Agency Solution (Paid).

 **Don't FORGET!** You can find a detailed comparison of HootSuite versus MavSocial at this link: *https://www.getapp.com/marketing-software/a/hootsuite/compare/mavsocial/*

ZOHO SOCIAL

ZOHO Social is yet another tool that has made its name in the social media management domain. It facilitates businesses to analyze and monitor revenue from social media campaigns, automate and schedule social media posts, and manage multiple social profiles in a seamless manner. Similar to Hootsuite, it provides a dashboard to work with these features.

Zoho Social has a prediction engine that helps determine the ideal time to publish posts to get greater visibility. It also provides features that assist in engaging with customers. Zoho Social includes ready-made or custom reporting tools for improved performance.

You can monitor the data to keep track of what people say about your brands. Team members can collaborate and discuss on reports. Scheduling of posts can be done across time zones, and also factor in daylight savings. Digital and social media agencies can fortify their brand by customizing Zoho Social with their own agency logo, domain name, and so on.

Who is Using Zoho Social?

Century 21, Novare Education, Pemco, and Table Top Records are some of the companies using ZohoSocial.

Zoho Social Pricing Plans

Zoho Social offers a free edition and two priced plans, each for businesses and agencies: Standard and Professional.

>  You can find a detailed comparison of HootSuite versus Zoho Social at this link: **https://www.getapp. com/marketing-software/a/hootsuite/compare/ zoho-social/**

If This Then That

IFTTT is a free cloud service that connects two apps to complete a task on one app based on the condition on the other app. Also called as **If-This-Then-That (IFTTT),** this process works as a conditional utility.

You can choose from readymade recipes or customize your own. Customizing doesn't require any special skillsets or deep technical knowhow. It can be used as a social media management tool by connecting two social media apps or sites together.

For example, consider that you want to connect your Facebook and Twitter profiles and want to automate some actions. Suppose you want to automatically change your Twitter profile pic whenever you update your Facebook photo or tweet your Facebook status updates when it changes. You can automate these actions through IFTTT recipes. Once you sign up for free, you can browse through a vast collection of pre-existing recipes.

IFTTT is available across Android, iOS, Google, and Windows platforms.

IFTTT Pricing

It is free to use.

SOCIALPILOT

SocialPilot is a social media management tool exclusively created for agencies and social media professionals.

Following are the features of SocialPilot:

- Helps share as many as 500 posts and link them to as many as 200 social profiles from one account
- Does not impose character limits on social media posts
- Helps perform social media analytics
- Enables bulk scheduling of posts
- Is affordable for businesses and agencies

Social Pilot Pricing Plans

SocialPilot offers a free plan, four paid plans and a 14-day free trial for each paid package.

 TweetDeck

TweetDeck is a social media management tool exclusively for Twitter. It cannot work with any other social media platforms. It allows a Twitter user to manage multiple Twitter accounts simultaneously from a unified interface. Businesses can leverage it for real-time tracking and to manage their brand profiles on Twitter. Originally created as an independent app, it was later acquired by Twitter Inc. and incorporated into Twitter's interface.

TweetDeck helps to manage and organize unlimited number of Twitter accounts. You can monitor lists, hashtags, searches, and so on through a single unified dashboard. TweetDeck provides users customizable social media dashboards that allow them to send and receive tweets aside from managing and monitoring Twitter profiles.

According to Twitter, TweetDeck is the most popular Twitter application to date. TweetDeck can be deployed as a Web app, a Chrome app, or a desktop app.

TweetDeck offers flexibility in terms of building and managing a list following, message tracking, scheduling and analytics, tweet filters, and so on. Users can also mark tweets as read. This can help greatly when users are tracking multiple accounts and there is an overload of tweets and feeds.

TweetDeck is available as a Web app, a Chrome app, and a desktop app.

TweetDeck Pricing

TweetDeck is a freeware application.

≋ buffer

Buffer is another online social media management tool. Instead of traditionally logging in on Facebook, LinkedIn, Twitter, Google+, and other social media sites, Buffer can connect to all at once. It also enables users to create posts and upload them with a single click. Browser extensions for Buffer are available for seamless integration with WordPress, Safari, Chrome, Firefox, RSS readers, and other important tools.

Buffer provides an organized layout with options available in its UI to add social media networks such as most notably Twitter, Facebook, and LinkedIn.

Users can schedule posts for later with the **Add to Buffer** option. The app decides when it can publish the post.

Embedded analytics offers data on number of clicks, mentions received, retweets, and potential reach of a user's posts. This can help businesses track their social media marketing.

Buffer Pricing Plans

Individual – Free, Awesome, Small, Medium, and Large

AgoraPulse is a user-friendly social community and moderation tool that helps business, manage social network profile on platforms such as Facebook, Twitter, Instagram, LinkedIn, and Google Plus.

AgoraPulse also comes with additional tools to help businesses, obtain critical data such as statistics and reporting. This can aid their social media marketing strategy. It allows to publish content, reply to tweets, share pictures on Facebook, schedule Twitter posts for later updation and more. AgoraPulse lets businesses view how many comments, messages and tweets their accounts have received. A single, centralized dashboard displays all the data.

AgoraPulse Pricing Plans

It offers four payment plans to suit needs of different users: Small, Medium, Large, and Enterprise. All of which are paid plans.

sproutsocial

Sprout Social is a SaaS based software that helps manage social communication.

Similar to the other tools discussed, Sprout Social offers a well-organized dashboard. In this case, the subject area on the dashboard is divided into six sections: Messages, Tasks, Feed, Publishing, Discovery, and Reports.

Sprout Social Pricing

It offers three different plans Premium, Corporate, and Enterprise for its users and each of the plans includes a 30-day free trial.

Table 10.1 summarizes the features of each of these tools.

Social Media Tool	Dashboard	Free Trial/ Free Plan	Browser Based/ Extension	Mobile App	Scheduling	Social Analytics
Agora Pulse	✓	✓ (15 days trial)	✓	✓	✓	✓
Buffer	✓	✓ (free forever + paid plans)	✓	✓	✓	✓
Hoot Suite	✓	✓ (30 day free trial + paid plans)	✓	✓	✓	✓

IFTTT	✓	✓(free forever)	✓	✓	✓	✓
MAV Social	✓	✓ (30 day free trial + paid plans)	✓	✓	✓	✓
Social Pilot	✓	✓(14 day trial	✓	✓	✓	✓
Sprout Social	✓	✓ (30 day free trial + paid plans)	✓	✓	✓	✓
Tweet Deck	✓	✓ (free forever)	✓	✓	✓	✓
Zoho Social	✓	✓ (free edition + paid editions)	✓	✓	✓	✓

Table 10.1

Summary

- Social media management tools facilitate operations such as quick response to feedback, gathering vital information from followers, gathering data on customer behavior and satisfaction, and soon.

- Some popular social media management tools today include HootSuite, MAV Social, Zoho Social, IFTTT, Social Pilot, TweetDeck, Buffer, AgoraPulse, and SproutSocial.

- Hootsuite is a social media management tool that helps businesses plan, and implement outstanding social media strategies.

- MavSocial is a social media management tool that includes content curation, scheduling and automation of social media posts, managing social media interactions, and more. MavSocial helps makes it easier for you to publish visual content.

- ZOHO Social facilitates businesses to analyze and monitor revenue from social media campaigns, automate and schedule social media posts, and manage multiple social profiles in a seamless manner.

- IFTTT is a free cloud service that connects two apps to complete a task on one app based on the condition on the other app.

- SocialPilot is a social media management tool exclusively created for agencies and social media professionals.

- TweetDeck is a social media management tool exclusively for Twitter and allows a Twitter user to manage multiple Twitter accounts simultaneously from a unified interface.

- Buffer is an Internet-based app intended for managing social media content. Instead of traditionally logging in on Facebook, LinkedIn, Twitter, Google+, and other social media sites, Buffer will do it all at once.

- AgoraPulse is a social community and moderation tool that helps business manage all their social network profiles.

- Sprout Social is a SaaS based software that helps manage social communication.

Chapter 10 Quiz

1. Which of these tools is completely free to use? (Select al that apply)

   A. SproutSocial   B. AgoraPulse
   C. TweetDeck   D. IFTTT

2. Which of these tools helps make it easier for you to publish visual content by making available over 70 million royalty-free images?

   A. MavSocial   B. SproutSocial
   C. AgoraPulse   D. TweetDeck

3. _____ is a social media management tool exclusively for Twitter.

Appendix A
Other Social Media Tools

* ❖ **Telegram** *(https://web.telegram.org/)*
* ❖ **Viber** *(https://www.viber.com/)*
* ❖ **Hike Messenger** *(http://www.hike.in)*
* ❖ **WeChat** *(https://web.wechat.com/)*
* ❖ **LINE** *(https://line.me/download)*

Appendix B
Reference Links

Social Media Marketing:

https://searchengineland.com/guide/what-is-social-media-marketing

https://smallbiztrends.com/2018/10/15-social-media-marketing-strategies-the-pros-use.html

https://sproutsocial.com/insights/social-media-marketing-strategy/

ANSWER KEYS

Chapter 1 Quiz

1. False
2. Advanced Research Projects AgencyNetwork
3. Synchronous
4. Non-verbal

Chapter 2 Quiz

1. True
2. True
3. False

Chapter 3 Quiz

1. False
2. True
3. ICQ
4. Sixdegrees.com
5. True

Chapter 4 Quiz

1. True
2. False
3. True
4. Bookmarks
5. Like

Chapter 5 Quiz

1. False
2. True
3. False
4. True
5. False

Chapter 6 Quiz

1. A
2. 100 MB
3. True

Chapter 7 Quiz

1. True
2. False
3. True
4. True

Chapter 8 Quiz

1. C
2. D
3. D
4. False
5. True

Chapter 9 Quiz

1. False
2. False
3. Messaging
4. True
5. True

Chapter 10 Quiz

1. C and D
2. A
3. TweetDeck

Printed in Great Britain
by Amazon